I Did It!

*16 Mindset Secrets To Transform
The Life You Have Into
The Ultimate Life You Deserve*

TRILBY JOHNSON

First published by Kleo Merrick 2020

Copyright © 2020 Individual Authors

ISBN
978-1-922506-03-0 (paperback)
978-1-922506-04-7 (ebook)

This work is copyright. Apart from any use permitted under the *Copyright Act 1968*, no part of this publication may be reproduced, stored in a retrieval system or transmitted in any form or by any means, electronic, mechanical, photocopying, recording or otherwise, without the prior written permission of each author.

Layout and typesetting: Busybird Publishing

Busybird Publishing
2/118 Para Road
Montmorency, Victoria
Australia 3094
www.busybird.com.au

Testimonials

Sophia Rigas

Sophia, I admire the fact that you were strong enough to start all over and stand on your own two feet. That takes courage, or as you say, M&Ms.

José

Living through hardships and maintaining dignity and a sense of humour is rare. To have emerged anew with vivacity and self-knowledge is exceptional.

Alexandra

A very tasty analogy! What a pleasure to read the ups and downs of your incredible journey. Very inspirational.

Katharine

Martin Probst

Martin's strategies are easily relatable and create a huge positive impact on businesses, teams and individuals. No matter what stage of your career or success, Martin's guide to big changes will help you achieve the right positive mindset.

Kerry Brocks – CEO & Founder of the Asia Pacific Institute of Learning & Performance, Queensland, Australia

Martin's story and his wisdom provide you with different perspectives and choices in your personal and professional life. Applying his strategies are a real game-changer.

David Hailstones, FIH, MBA – CEO & Chief Culture Officer at Swiss Institute for Management & Hospitality, Lucerne, Switzerland

In this inspirational chapter, Martin Probst shares his amazing story and, in his own remarkable voice, he provides us with both the mindset lessons from his life's journey and a pathway and mindset tactics to Transform the Life We Have into the Ultimate Life We Desire.

Bill Jarrard, MEI ILPF CLF – Co-Founder, Mindwerx International, Melbourne, Australia

Trilby Johnson

Trilby's words flow off the page seamlessly. It made me think about who I am – am I serving myself truly? Trilby is inspiring and is honest about her struggles and achievements in her endeavour to find herself and contentment.

Fliss Austin – Naturopath, New Zealand

Trilby shows you how you can go from not loving yourself to really appreciating your way of thinking and your body. She shows you different methods you can use and that can help you on your amazing personal inner journey and the joy and freedom you can finally find.

Erika Reber – Switzerland

Trilby Johnson's writing style is always flowing, an "easy read". In this chapter, I found myself being carried along, as if floating down a stream. Trilby speaks of issues I can identify with, and even in this short piece, the wisdom of her experiences shines. I look forward to more.

Bonnie Bonsor – U.S.A.

Terri Tonkin

An inspiring read, how mindset can really kick some major goals for yourself. Starting with an idea transforming into an enjoyable passion with health benefits!

Wendy Trevarthen – Health and Wellness Coach; Healthy Options Now; Brisbane, Australia

An inspirational story of Terri's journey from a sometime walker, to a jogger, through to a competitive runner of half marathons, at a time in her life when many are retiring from physical sports. The steps to her success can be applied to any goal we could wish to set. We just have to take the first step.

Joyce Homer – Bundaberg, Australia

Terri's story of grit and determination is an inspiring and uplifting journey from what started as an idea to a constant and consistent focus on her goal. An inspiring chapter on the power of a strong mindset.

Suzanne Duncan – Certified Mindset & Behavioural Coach | Author | Team & Individual Workplace Coach | Behavioural Assessment Profile; Discovery Within; Melbourne, Australia

Maylin Lim

Maylin has an authenticity of her processes as she applies them sincerely to herself first; she models her work. She has worked on her own evolution deeply and humbly and now offers gold to those of us seeking growth and healing."

Wendy Stuart – Wendy & Words

WOW!! My direct experience is Maylin's is a MASTER HEALER. I'm a 37-year veteran of personal growth, I know a master when I see one. I've witnessed part of her transformation as she cleared deep root causal pain. Maylin is inspiring, encouraging & vulnerable.

Satina Cooper

It took great courage to relate the raw details of Maylin's experience, the inspiration that she gained from successfully overcoming her painful childhood experiences and transforming herself into a peaceful and joyful woman. Maylin's skill lies in communicating a deep spirituality in every interaction with people. She lifts you up.

Vicky Mangels

Carol Davies

I was totally engrossed in the emotional roller-coaster journey Carol takes you on in her captivating 10 steps to handle changes in our lives. The key inspirational message of finding your true self was encompassed in this powerful sentence: "every time you step into self-doubt you give away your power".

Peter Beckenham – The Village Marketer, Thailand

Carol's gift is answering the pivotal questions around, "Where do I start?" "What is my passion?" finding the solution by defining the steps she took and, highlighting the ways to finding our true authentic self, thus demonstrating the joy of finding self-confidence and self-esteem, to become the best you can be.

Linda Curtis – Author, Speaker at Wow the Now@Sixty Plus Success, Morpeth, UK

I was really moved by Carol's struggles throughout her life. I felt myself traveling beside her all the way. It stirred up a lot of emotions and thoughts that I have had throughout my life. I have worked with Carol and her positivity and outlook on life has had a profound effect on me.

Kellie Doiron – Wellness Shopping Coach, Oshawa, ON Canada

Cheryl Strickland

I love the different strategies Cheryl used. My only comment is "Why could I have not read this chapter prior to this happening to me?" I feel if I had this info I might not have been as hard on myself as I was during that dark time in my life. Thank you for your advice.

Kellie Doiron – Wellness Shopping Coach, Oshawa, Ontario, Canada

When Cheryl's job became redundant she had the choice of giving into a victim mentality or accepting what had happened and then looking at all the options to find "an amazing new future". Cheryl's tenacity drove a "can do" approach and her strong message is "there's no time to waste" by focusing on the negative.

Linda Curtis – Author, Speaker, with Wow the Now@Sixty Plus Success, Morpeth, UK

An excellent story that highlighted the traumas of losing control of your personal and work life due to redundancy. I would endorse the five steps to developing the growth mind-set and never give up.

Duncan J. McKay – Independent Data Management Consultant, Aberdeen (Scotland)

Kleo Merrick

Kleo writes in a way that is relatable and confronting. I felt so many moments of familiarity because I know exactly how it feels to be this way; to be a pleaser, and to constantly seek approval from others. Coming to terms with being this way and admitting it is the hardest part in the healing process, and Kleo has described the sensations involved perfectly!

Olga Makarios

Kleo certainly gives you food for thought, it makes you look at and think about your own lifestyle choices.

Jane Featherstone

Kleo has an inspirational message for all to hear. Her words describe how many of us feel but don't fully understand what is occurring. Thank you for lifting the lid for others to discover what is underlying.

Teressa Todd – Burleigh, Australia.

Kerry Cleopatra

Love. The quintessential desire of every human being, yet this force of nature is often poorly understood. Kerry Cleopatra has written a most articulate and heartwarming account of the principles that comprise the life-art of love. A must read for anyone willing to truly embody being love.

Simone M. Matthews – founder Spiritual Lightrition & UniversalLifeTools.com

Kerry's passion to inspire and empower others is second to none. Her lived experience and nourishing words travel deep into the soul's depths in order to help you blossom from inside out.

Grace Love – Visionary & Hypno-Psychotherapist

Beautifully written, powerful in its message and a Gift to those who forget the truth of who we really are (and who doesn't!). A wonderful chapter of clarity, love and remembrances.

Diane McCann – Director of 'Beyond The Ordinary'

Suzanne Duncan

We can never predict what life is going to throw at us, but in this chapter, Suzanne – through her own remarkable journey – shows that we have choices about how we respond, how we stand up in the difficult times and how we choose to react – by taking ownership of our own transformational journey from within.

Jake Adam Davey – Instagram Marketing Expert. Manchester, UK.

Testimonials continued on pg 155

Contents

Chapter One - *Trilby Johnson*
Becoming Believably Me							3

Chapter Two - *Teressa Todd*
A Journey from Within							13

Chapter Three - *Kleo Merrick*
The True Confessions of an Unresourceful Rescuer			23

Chapter Four - *Joslyn A Gardiner*
Your LIFE, Your CHOICE!						33

Chapter Five - *Scott Lawrence*
Rejection Can't Kill You						43

Chapter Six - *Kitiboni Rolle Adderley*
Navigating the Waves							51

Chapter Seven - *Carol Davies*
The Joy of Finding Self-Confidence and Self-Esteem			61

Chapter Eight - *Maylin Lim*
How to Reconnect With Your Life Purpose After Abandonment	71

Chapter Nine - *Petros Galanoulis*
The Greatest Lesson I Learned as a Coach				79

Chapter Ten - *Sally Holden*
Life Woke Me Up							89

Chapter Eleven - *Sophia Rigas*
My Life as a Jelly Bean							99

Chapter Twelve - *Cheryl Strickland*
Perseverance, Resilience and the Growth Mindset – A Key Trio	105

Chapter Thirteen - *Suzanne Duncan*
Leading Well From Within						115

Chapter Fourteen - *Kerry Cleopatra*
Becoming love								125

Chapter Fifteen - *Martin Probst*
Empowerment – The Greatest Strength Comes From Within	135

Chapter Sixteen - *Terri Tonkin*
I Can Run								145

Introduction

"I did it, Mummy!" Alexia exclaimed. My three-year-old daughter was playing with her puzzle box and had managed to open the wooden lid with a slide mechanism, all by herself. I watched her as she went from a state of very serious, focused and frowning concentration to a state of complete joy and elation in a matter of moments.

After praising her for her amazing achievement, I thought to myself – as adults we don't do that for ourselves enough. Firstly, the praising part – we don't do this for the fear of looking silly, so we settle to downplay everything we achieve and play it safe in our community.

Secondly, the announcing of it! It's only a simple declaration of achievement – yet sharing it with others can feel so wrong …

We, as individuals, parents, grandparents, business owners, employees, etc., do not praise ourselves enough for all of our magnificent achievements – even for the most simple and basic steps forward. And more often than not, because of the fear of judgement, we are all petrified to proclaim: *I Did It!*

Personally, I'm sick of this! I want this idea to leave the shadows once and for all and finally step into the light, and be seen in all its glory.

Because, you know what? No matter what you do or achieve in this world, no matter how big or how small your challenges may be, someone else in this world is petrified about taking exactly that same step as you. And they desperately need your help.

So, what if you could share? What if you could tell them and spread the message of your achievements or "challenge over-comings" to the world for the people that needed to hear it?

This is what myself and my amazing collaborators have hoped to achieve by sharing our stories with you in this book.

> *"Taking the first step takes Courage …*
> *Taking the second step takes Conviction …*
> *Taking the third step takes Determination …*
> *All steps after this take pure Passion …"*
> – *Kleo Merrick*

In this book I'm privileged to be joined by:

Sophia Rigas, Petros Galanoulis, Trilby Johnson, Scott Lawrence, Kerry Cleopatra, Teressa Todd, Suzanne Duncan, Martin Probst, Sally Holden, Terri Tonkin, Maylin Lim, Carol Davies, Cheryl Strickland, Joslyn Gardiner and Kitiboni Rolle Adderley.

We, as a collective, are excited to share our personal journeys with you. In the hope that reading ours will help you grow, learn, develop, challenge and most importantly overcome your own battles.

To be able to stand tall and declare to the world – "I Did It!"

With love and gratitude,

Kleo Merrick xxx

Chapter One

Becoming Believably Me
by Trilby Johnson

Breakthrough Healer and Mentor, Best-Selling Author and Speaker, New Zealand

"The longest journey you will make in your life is from your head to your heart."
– Sioux legend

For many years of my life, every time I heard someone say, "It's better to give than to receive," I honestly felt uncomfortable. I would get this knot in the pit of my stomach and a feeling that I was missing something. You see, like the good little girl and daughter I was trying to be, I was playing at being NICE. I thought if I was nice enough people would like me more and would find me worthy.

It felt like there was something terribly wrong or broken within me. And I would find myself giving and giving, usually ending up feeling angry and resentful. This would be followed by bouts of guilt, shame and self-doubt. So for many years, to make up for these low feelings, I would try being even NICER to the detriment of myself.

I felt like I was on an emotional runaway train, heading for my doom and I didn't know how to stop. Things got so bad that contemplating suicide appeared to be the better option and solution. My mental health was under attack and very fragile!

Fortunately, one day, I experience a shift within. My rebellious streak stirred and I realised that rocking the boat was a better alternative to suicide. Albeit one that required extreme courage and risking being judged, ostracised and rejected. This shift in perception reminded me how resilient the human spirit is.

Life itself proved to be a great teacher – once I understood the lessons, that is! Even when I was young, I was a keen observer of people and situations. I noticed things instinctively, that most others didn't. I could feel whether things were okay or not, whether someone was angry or sad, lying or being honest, and whether they liked me or not. I didn't always understand, however, and struggled, often judging myself instead.

I was aware of so much suffering and struggle around me. In my young heart, I knew that there was much more to life. However, it wasn't until my mid-twenties that things became clearer, when I heard the term "Empath".

An Empath is someone who's highly sensitive to all events, in particular other people's emotions or thoughts. They can sense a multitude of vibrations and feel overwhelmed due to the enormous influx of sensorial information. It takes skill to learn to discern between tuning in to their own perceptions, or tapping into other stimuli, from their surroundings and/or other people's.

Always curious, I was an avid reader and I can say that books proved my best friends and probably saved my life growing up. Within the pages of books, I discovered and uncovered new worlds that seemed filled with the magic and knowledge I was seeking and that was absent in my own direct reality.

It took several more years to learn how to hone the life skills necessary to successfully manage my own energy and differentiate from the overload of sensorial information that bombarded me and to stand confidently and calmly.

With this breakthrough, rather than the accustomed feelings of being overwhelmed, drained, unappreciated and resentful, I slowly began to know how to distinguish and honour my own feelings and needs from those of others in healthier and happier ways.

Over time, I felt more assertive and comfortable in my own self-worth and I made a conscious choice to believe in me, and perhaps more significantly, to feel safe doing this!

It didn't happen overnight and it took several attempts. And then, there were more days, when I would wake up and the pain and lack of confidence was receding. It began to be replaced by a feeling of inner harmony and outer balance.

Thankfully, I turned a corner and began to experience the benefits of choosing to be believably me. What helped me was understanding these few things:

- Life is precious and too short to spend doing unfulfilling things and not feeling enjoyment.
- No matter what others think, at the end of the day, I live with myself and want to feel good about who I am.
- My intuition has never let me down.
- My "self-worth" is a given and not something I needed to earn.
- I naturally love and believe in myself, that's the reason I felt so bad when I doubted myself and believed others more than my inner wisdom.
- It's safe to be me.

So, what helped me to break through and create the shift from giving away myself and feeling insecure and inadequate, to being believably me with confidence and enjoyment?

There was no quick fix, and yet with hindsight I can say that it was much simpler than I made it. I also really wanted my life to change. It took a lot of courage, determination and perseverance, especially at first. And I did it!

There were several things I implemented to create new habits and behaviours that supported me in becoming believably me.

Meditation

I always felt more comfortable in the world of energy than this reality, so meditation was like fresh air to me. Looking back, I can see how the practice of mediation really provided an essential foundation.

I read a lot and tried many types of meditation before I found a combination that worked for me. In our busy lives, it is vital to have time for self-connection each day.

Meditation taught me detachment from my thoughts and emotions and offered a safe space in which to release and integrate my own wisdom and discernment. It enabled me to feel connected to something bigger that felt peaceful, wiser, free of judgment and real.

Meditation allows the brain the time it needs to slow down and integrate all the information coming our way and without this practice in my life, I probably wouldn't be around today. When meditating, there is no doubt about who I am.

Conscious Breathing

The benefits of the breath are often overlooked, misunderstood and understated. It is the simplest and quickest way to feel connected, calmer and be present and grounded in your body. It can be done anywhere – as you're doing it anyway – without anyone noticing anything unusual. And it can make all the difference in how to handle a situation.

When I was studying psychology, I experienced exam anxiety for the first time when revising. I took medication, with little improvement. Fortunately, my course tutor suggested a simple breathing technique that helped. This changed everything!

I experienced the instant transformative power of the breath to calm the mind and lower the heart rate and to cut through the sense of panic – purposefully!

I have found that some deep breathing helped me to feel more assertive and poised when it came to saying "no", whether in a private or professional interaction. As if by magic, the other person also seemed to accept my decision with more ease and less resistance.

The breath itself, offered me insight into my hang up with giving … A breath is an inhalation AND an exhalation. This is one breath! And when I give … I receive … and vice versa.

The breath is the key to fulfilment and we are the vessels.

Mindset

When it comes to thought quality and control, I choose to be the master of my thoughts rather than be at their whim. This was one of the most impactful learnings I had – I am not my thoughts.

I can choose the kind of thoughts I want to think. I can choose where I want to focus and how. In my experience, there has to be a balance of beliefs AND values to create a mindset that is successful and feels fulfilling.

Mindset has to feel good in the long run, otherwise, and regardless of how good it is, it loses momentum. It's not merely a mental construct. It's an emotional construct too – something that's often overlooked in mindset techniques.

For instance, even although I did believe in myself to some degree, for me to be believably me, I had to feel safe to do this. Until, I recognised that feeling safe was an important value to me, I didn't fully believe.

For a mindset to be effectively implemented, it needs to align with your value system. After all, humans need meaning to help make sense of life.

Be Okay Feeling Uncomfortable

When you first step out of your comfort zone and into new areas, it's going to feel uncomfortable and off balance for a period, as you try out new things and meet new people.

Give yourself permission and some slack to explore different states. What really helped me to change, stick to my guns and say "no" and mean it, was choosing to stop dishonouring myself at the expense of others.

I would often do things because I felt that it was expected of me and so I did, as I was afraid of doing something wrong. What I noticed, though, was that when I did things and felt this way about them, the experience never went well. What was excruciating was the emotional pain and shame I felt repeatedly for letting myself down.

Over time, it was this lack of support for myself that began eroding at my confidence and self-trust. This way of operating was not working for me and I began taking note of how I felt when thinking about certain events. The feeling of resentment for instance became a sure sign that somewhere, I was not in alignment with what I truly desire. I started asking myself questions.

Did I really want to go, or was I just going because I didn't want to rock the boat? If I didn't really want to go, I would say, "no, thanks."

Soon, I noticed that I actually enjoyed myself more when I didn't go or when I did. I realised that when I honoured myself, I was actually allowing others to empower themselves.

I made a commitment to stop lying and letting myself down. There is no way you can ever run far enough to get away from yourself, so best to stop and embrace yourself and become your own best friend.

Self-Care

My best friend is my body and it's my first home! This is a surprising statement considering that for much of my younger years I struggled with acute low body image and genuinely felt my physical appearance was to blame for my unhappiness.

Nevertheless, no matter how much self-loathing, judgment, abuse, emotional eating and forced exercise I heaped on my body, my body faithfully kept me going and guided me.

It has kept me on track, constantly taking care of me above and beyond my limited thinking. No social norm can ever give me or do for me even half of what my body does for me on a daily basis.

When I chose to love my body, guess what happened? It responded rapidly with gifts of feeling good, happy and healthy.

So, take care of your body. It's the most sophisticated technology you'll ever have. Feed it good food when it's hungry. Ask it what it requires, rather than forcing it to do unwanted tasks.

So many people punish their body with strict exercise and diet regimes. Enjoy your body! Find ways to feel comfortable in it and with it. It's your home.

Mentoring

I could not have achieved the personal growth I have on my own, without reaching out to others for assistance and expertise. Even experts like Richard Branson, Joe Despenza have had their mentors along the way.

A professional and qualified facilitator or mentor can support you unbiasedly and assist you in uncovering and transforming your blind spots.

Having a mentor, ensures your own ongoing growth, stimulation and motivation.

There is something powerful in the dynamic of working with someone who is fully supportive of you! They can challenge you to become more than you may currently believe you are capable of, in a way that is safe and honouring of you.

Find someone who inspires you and has life skills you want to acquire and who leaves you feeling qualified to manage your life, on your terms.

Learn from their experience and knowledge and adapt it to suit your lifestyle and aspirations.

The only part of your life that you do solo is actually to choose your attitude about something. Your attitude can be compared to a pair of glasses that you can put on, take off or change when you look at things. They change the way you see or rather perceive things and the action that you then choose to make and take.

Everything else is about cooperation and for that you need the power of two or more. I believe that's how we can support each other – by sharing and expressing our talents and skills.

When you are ready and prepared to create a change in your life, ask to be shown the perfect solution and person. Then allow it to show up and be discerning in your choice.

In Closing

I knew I had done it, when my life finally shifted from one of despair, self-loathing, resentment, lack and feeling not good enough. Today, I feel safe being believably me. And I love who I was and who I am and will be!

Feeling this way about myself, I am more prone to "gifting" from a place of enjoyment, rather than from the earlier sense of duty that didn't serve anyone. Perhaps more importantly, I have learned to be compassionate and to enjoy my life.

The greatest gift I offered myself was to really feel my belief in myself and to trust this! In my experience, this is how to give with ease and joy … Life gives back what we offer. So it's a win-win, don't you think?

It's only possible to receive in life what you are willing to give and feel good doing!

When I realised this, I was able to release my ambivalence around giving. Giving and receiving are two sides of the very same coin. Both are required and afford the experience of inner harmony and outer balance.

It meant consciously choosing and being willing to experience, what it means that "everything is within!" To believe and know – I am whole, worthy and enough – period!

Freedom came with the understanding that the events and people that showed up in my life were intimately linked to my dominant beliefs and values. My strength lies in choosing to believe in ways that uplift and expand and that meet my personal values.

Fortunately, I realised the connection between my inner world and emotions and what was showing up externally. I claimed my natural birthright of being worthy and enough.

I chose to feel safe and be believably me, no matter what.

I DID IT! And so can you.

> *"There is no identity in Freedom."*
> *– Trilby Johnson, A-Ha Moments*

In appreciation and love,

Trilby Johnson

About the Author

Trilby Johnson is a breakthrough mentor, intuitive healer, best-selling author and speaker. Her clients love the inner shifts of awareness she facilitates for them and the practical life skills she teaches, so they experience inner harmony and outer balance in their lives, relationships, finances, health, mindset and soul connection.

Trilby runs her successful business – Trilby Johnson: The Connective – from New Zealand, with online and in person sessions. With a foot in the corporate world for three decades, Trilby simultaneously followed her passion for knowledge and personal growth. She has a Bachelor of Science Honours Degree in Psychology and qualifications in Biochemical Therapy, Reiki, Neurolinguistic Programming, DNA Activation, Holistic Massage Therapy, Meta-Coaching and numerous Advanced Bodywork.

As a best-selling author, her transformational books available are Voices of the 21st Century, Fearlessly Alone – Find Your Happy No Matter What and A-Ha Moments – Inspirational Quotes to Shift Your Thinking.

Trilby loves life, travelling, reading, writing, nature, enjoying good food and time with great people.

Trilby Johnson: The Connective

Website: https://www.trilbyjohnsontheconnective.com
Facebook: www.facebook.com/trilbytheconnective
Instagram: www.instagram.com/trilbytheconnective
LinkedIn: www.linkedin.com/in/trilby-johnson
Twitter: www.twitter.com/connectivebody
YouTube: www.youtube.com/c/Trilbyjohnsontheconnective

Dedication

To Mom, in loving memory! You taught me a love of the sea, books and avocados. Love you always.

Chapter Two

A Journey from Within
by Teressa Todd

Australia's #1 Naturopath, Biochemist and Microbiologist, Australia

"Health and wellbeing are more than no disease. It is about how you live your life through the triumphs and the struggles. Life is what you make of it. The best part of health is the options it grants for."

– *Teressa Todd*

Following My Heart

It was never any different. Growing up I always wanted to be in a profession to help others. I was good at science and loved helping people, so following this interest into university to do a science degree was a natural step.

It was halfway through my science degree when my father saw a naturopath for his health and I loved how the profession encompassed everything about the whole body and included the concept of eating for health. Naturopathy seemed like a natural choice for me.

After finishing my first degree I went to find a university that offered naturopathy. I was so committed to undertake this course that I drove two and a half hours each way to and from university to attend the only university in Australia that taught the Bachelor of Naturopathy.

The drive and ambition to keep learning stemmed from my mother. She had a childhood that didn't offer many opportunities and she didn't get to achieve her aspirations in younger life. Due to her life struggles, mum instilled in me a determination to achieve my desires.

After graduating from my naturopathy course, I worked in health food shops, pharmacies and chiropractic clinics to acquire hands-on experience and refine my skills, feeling that I was contributing to the health of others.

Taking Life for Granted

Looking back at my childhood I would sum it up as a fortunate childhood.

My activities during childhood revolved around school and equestrianism, primarily in dressage and eventing. My horses and I became state and interschool champions.

Equestrianism was an avenue for me to be competitive. It was a competition within myself. There was a drive to be the best that I could be at all times. This internal drive can sometimes result in placing too much pressure on myself.

Throughout childhood, I saw my parents run their own successful family business. This was my first introduction to running a business and it gave me the belief that I could do it too.

However, they created success that I took for granted. Looking back, I see that they worked very hard to give my sister and me many opportunities. Dad would sometimes work nights and weekends, and mum would stay up late at night doing the bookwork for the business. Even though she did this, mum was always there for the family. This is a quality I admire.

From this, I reasoned that running your own business gave the flexibility to work your own hours. So, unconsciously, I decided that I wanted my own business during life.

Then things changed …

Tough Challenges Ahead

A few years after my graduation and entering working life in naturopathy, I met my husband. At this stage, I was not thinking that I would want a family and marriage, but that changed. They say things change when you meet Mr Right.

When I met my husband, I knew that he had been diagnosed with multiple sclerosis, but it certainly didn't stop him from living his life. Together, we built a health clinic. Once the clinic was thriving, it was time to start our own family and pregnancy followed.

During my pregnancy, my mum was diagnosed with Parkinson's disease and dementia. That was a hard blow!

Mum had been a strength throughout my life and now I had to be there for her – making financial and life decisions for her at a time when I should have been basking in my first pregnancy.

One day at the hospital with Mum, while I was heavily pregnant, I remember feeling so overwhelmed that I desperately wished things were different. That life was different. That things were easier. I was struggling with the demands of the pregnancy and the emotions of watching a woman, who had always been a tower of strength, decline in front of me. I didn't know what to do. She was no longer the mum I knew and at a time when I needed her the most. I didn't know where to turn to or what to do. So, I buried the emotions and moved on.

Soon after the birth of my daughter, my first personal health challenge occurred.

One day I saw my reflection and saw a lump in my throat. I knew that underactive thyroid function was common in many women post-pregnancy. That is what I thought it was. It turned out to be more. I was diagnosed with thyroid cancer and an autoimmune disease.

I never had any symptoms. I felt crushed.

I had a three month-old baby who I wanted to see grow up.

When you hear the C-word, emotions take over and the mind doesn't think straight. The only way I could deal with this and not let fear take over was to think of it as a growth, rather than cancer. My mind could handle the situation better thinking this way. I wasn't being naive but rather not succumbing to the emotion and thought processes associated with cancer.

The next big life challenge arose concerning my husband's health a year later.

A combination of back surgery, multiple viral infections and stress crippled his immune system and re-triggered his multiple sclerosis. He had been doing amazing before this but now his health went downhill. His health would improve, then decline, then improve and then decline again, it was a rollercoaster ride.

Now, I was watching my best friend struggle …

The World Around Me Was Crumbling

My world was falling apart. I felt like I was struggling through each day. I felt like I was failing as a wife. I was able to help clients with their health but battled with my husband's. I felt like it was my responsibility to fix him. I understand that everyone has their own life journey and life lessons, but I felt that this was my burden to fix. The pressure took a toll on me mentally and emotionally.

I began to doubt myself. I doubted my ability to guide others. I doubted myself as a wife and a mum. I realised that life was irreversibly changing. My mum had passed due to her illness, I now had two children under the age of seven, and a husband battling a degenerative condition. I felt alone.

My response was to throw myself into work so I could provide for my family, and work was a space that I could control. I couldn't control my husband's health, I couldn't control my mum's passing, but I could control my work.

Through this time, I was working so much that I started to burn out. I would get to the end of each year and be so fatigued. I was not following the principles that I taught to my clients. I was running off stress and stubbornness to keep going.

There had to be a different way to do this otherwise, I would wake up one day and not be able to be there for my family or my clients. It was important to find a plan that allowed me to work with my clients, support my family and create the flexibility for me to have time with my family.

I realised that I had to make changes in me. I may not have been able to control some things going on in life but I could control the path I took next …

Taking My Own Medicine

The first step was to make more time to exercise and make it a priority. I had always walked for fitness but now it was time to strengthen muscles and create physical flexibility. A flexible body connects with greater flexibility of the mind. Exercise helps reduce stress and increases endorphins (feel-good hormones).

Next was time for concerted rest and relaxation. I made sure that my time during the weekends was spent more with my family and less on household chores.

The following step involved following my heart (instinct) again. The same instinct that had guided me to become a naturopath.

Now was the time to reconnect.

If someone had told me in detail about my next experience I would have replied "Thanks, but no thanks."

You see, the next step took me on a path that was well outside my comfort zone. I had an urge to write a book. I signed up for a three-day book writing retreat. During the retreat, I was so nauseous from emotions that I couldn't eat. Who did I think I was to believe that I could write a book? Who would want to read it? I was doubting myself again.

I had to follow my instincts. I thought it was all too hard. I had to remember why I was doing this.

The process of writing the book became empowering for me. The concept of the book was to help the frazzled fatigued mums that needed guidance to restore energy and sanity, but quickly I realised that it was also helping me as well. It was everything I was doing in my life.

I had to go through this process to fully understand the impact of stress on others.

I had to step up and enlighten the path for others to see …

Ultimate Inspiration

As well as stepping up and writing a book, I attended a medical intuitive course. I enrolled to learn more tools to help with my husband's health. I had undertaken so many professional development courses over the years. This course is based on understanding the link between emotions and body imbalances. Day one started with standing up and saying why we were here. I stood up and being innately shy, I was nervous. As I stood up, I said, "I am here to help with my husband's health," then all of a sudden I continued, "but now I think I am here for me."

I was shocked by what came out.

That was not my intention.

Day one of the course I volunteered to be the example case. Oh my gosh, I never do this. I never put my hand up to be seen in courses. What was going on?

I was to be a case study for the group and during the process I felt tears flow. Usually, I would hold back my tears as I think that I need to be strong. This time I couldn't stop the tears. They flowed, I felt self-conscious.

The next day, the team and participants commented that I seemed different.

I felt different. Like a weight had been lifted.

It was the release of emotions that I had been storing, thinking that I had to be strong for everyone and not let anyone see that life wasn't textbook.

Now What?

I am still in the journey of dealing with life and the challenges that can be thrown at you. I am a different woman to who I used to be.

I feel stronger inside and I feel I have something to offer others, whether they know my story or not.

I feel greater strength to guide my children and promote a better future for them.

At the time of being diagnosed with thyroid cancer, I wouldn't refer to it as cancer. Instead, for over seven years I referred to it as a growth. My mind could handle that. Now, health professionals and researchers have studies to show how the mind and thoughts relate to illness.

The choice to refer to cancer as a growth formed part of my mindset and ability to be able to not get engulfed by fear. I believe that this helped me through without setbacks. I had surgery but no other treatment. Eleven years on I have had no repercussions.

You see, the body listens to what you think and if I allowed myself to think about "the cancer", then the fear and emotions would have compounded and my body would have understood that it was cancer and reacted as such and things could have turned out very differently.

Dr Bruce Lipton wrote a book *The Biology of Belief* and in it, he talks of how your thought influences your genetics and therefore your body function. I didn't read this book until nine years later but I had already used this concept.

I knew that I couldn't get dragged down by the thoughts that my body had cancer. This included any life situation I experienced.

If you want to grasp this concept, think of something you fear. For example, heights, skydiving or spiders. Now think of yourself in that situation. How is your body feeling? I bet your breathing rate changed and your muscles tensed up and a wave of emotion spread over you.

Well, that is your thoughts influencing your genes to alter your body's reactions. You produced stress hormones without being in the situation but just by thinking of the situation.

The thoughts influence your genes, which influences your health. The saying "your thoughts become you" is true.

Want to take control of your life? Take control of your thoughts!

Believe that you are in control!

Believe that you are not alone in this life, whatever the situation.

This is the concept that helped me.

Once I realised that I had a choice over my thoughts. I felt myself soar and that I can do this. I have this, I can conquer this! All is possible!

The Biggest Gift

I wanted to gift to you some of the principles that I have applied in my life:

1. Eat well to nourish your body. Enjoy a rainbow of colours of natural fruit and vegetables, with a balance of other food groups. You deserve to function on the best quality fuel.
2. Enjoy physical movement and activity. Combine your activity with strength, cardio and stretching to ensure all-round body health. This will help your mind, too!
3. Give yourself time for active rest and relaxation. It may involve meditation, yoga, massage, listening to music, reading a book or a hobby that you love to do. Take the time for yourself to recharge. Your body and mind will thank you for it!
4. Ask for help if you need to. It is ok. You are not alone. Ask a friend for help or seek a trusted health professional to listen to you and guide you.
5. Be aware of your thoughts. What you think becomes you. Awareness of your thoughts is the first step to being able to make a change. There is a saying that life is 10% what happens to you and 90% how you react. This is true.
6. You have the strength within you to deal with life and its challenges. Look within to see it. You are stronger than you think. Challenges are a way of showing us this inner strength.
7. Your health is your greatest asset – it encompasses mind, body and spirit. Use it wisely.

You are amazing, you are capable, you can do this, and together we show future generations the inner strength available to live their best life.

> *"From adversity, we realise our true strengths."*
> – Teressa Todd

Have a fabulous day,

TERESSA Todd

About the Author

Teressa Todd is a Naturopath, Biochemist, Microbiologist, author, speaker, business owner and practitioner. She has helped thousands of clients wanting to rebuild their health.

She is the author of *The Energy Solution – A Mothers' Guide to Go From Frazzled and Fatigued to Fabulous* and creator of her following signature programmes:

"Feeling Fabulous Program" – A six-week online programme that outlines easy-to-follow steps to support you from feeling frazzled and fatigued to feeling fabulous.

"Overcoming Autoimmune Disease Program" – A six-week online programme to discover the factors that play a role in autoimmune disease and the steps you can take to restore your health.

"Managing Menopause and Keeping Your Sanity Program" – This four-week online programme explains the changes that underpin menopause and the actions you can take to minimise your symptoms and maximise your life.

As Australia's first university-trained Naturopath, Biochemist and Microbiologist. Teressa's strength is in using evidence-based natural medicine approach and the ability to explain health concepts in easy-to-understand terms, enabling clients to regain their health.

> *"Teressa helped me understand what my body is doing (or should I say not doing). After months of not feeling well, I now have a plan of action!"*
> – Sandra M (Victoria, Australia)

Teressa is extremely passionate about helping you to get through your daily grind and optimise your health and wellbeing so that you can truly live your life to the fullest and enjoy time with your loved ones.

Teressa Todd – My Naturopath Gold Coast

Website: www.mynaturopathgoldcoast.com.au, www.teressatodd.com

Email: teressa@teresstodd.com

Facebook: https://www.facebook.com/TeressaToddNaturopath

Instagram: https://www.instagram.com/teressatoddnaturopath

LinkedIn: https://www.linkedin.com/in/teressatoddnaturopath/

Twitter: https://twitter.com/Teressa_Todd

Dedication

To my children, Sienna and Caylem, you are shining lights in my life and bring me so much joy and fun. Thank you for sharing this ride with me and creating beautiful memories together.

To my husband, Pete, my best friend and soulmate. You are an amazing, resilient man, who has been able to help me find my own strengths and beliefs. Thank you for all your support.

To my late mother, thank you for showing your strength and dedication so that I can dream big and accomplish my goals.

Chapter Three

The True Confessions of an Unresourceful Rescuer
by Kleo Merrick

#1 International Best-Selling Author, Speaker and Online Business Strategist, Melbourne, Australia

"The more challenges you face the easier they are to overcome."
– Kleo Merrick

I spent a lot of my childhood looking after other people.

My family owned a number of restaurants. I learned that looking after other people was a priority because they were the guests at our restaurants, and you had to look after them. For me, this was clear as crystal because if you didn't look after your customers and treat them right, you'd soon be out of business.

Unfortunately, what I *made it mean to me* was that I have to absolutely bend over backwards for everyone first to make sure that they were always happy and so they would like me. That would mean that they would come back to the restaurant and that my parents would be happy, and the business would be successful.

It also meant that I would be loved and accepted. That's how I led my life, not realising for years, that everything that I did – was for the approval of other people.

These beliefs, strategies and standards were carried through to adulthood and were all based on needing approval from others. If I didn't do things properly or if I made mistakes or made someone angry, that meant I didn't get the approval I was looking for. I believed I had failed, at work, at life and as a person, so I would have to compensate by putting in more time, more energy and make more of an effort.

Because of this, I would find myself constantly overcommitted. Always juggling fifty things and constantly dropping the ball, or as my old boss would tell me, "Letting things pass through to the keeper."

And it's all because I had the need to rescue everyone, everything and, in other words, control everything in my life and around me.

When I studied coaching, I discovered this was known as an *Unresourceful Rescuer*. By unresourceful, I mean that there is no way that it can be sustained, eventually something will give in, and in this instance, it was me.

What Is Unresourceful Rescuing?

I know you can understand this because you probably have experienced something similar or know someone like this.

As Unresourceful Rescuers, we spend most of our lives overworking to help others. If they don't actually want any help, we insist that we help them because we're a good friend. Then when they don't take our suggestions we crash and burn, get upset and feel disappointed. We become devastated because we think, "how can they not do what I said to them?" Because we really want to help and it's such a good idea and they really need to do it.

"Why can't they understand?"

We take it upon ourselves to rescue everyone and everything but ultimately what we're doing is creating a prison for ourselves. I spent so much of my life doing things to serve others that I forgot to do anything for myself.

It's a Trap

Fast forward to being an adult. I was exhausted, I had no direction in my life and this led to depression, stress and heavy drinking. I was lost and I had absolutely no idea what I wanted to do with my life. I didn't even have the understanding or believe that I could choose a different path from the one that I was on.

Then I stumbled across Life Coaching and from this I began my journey of self-discovery. It helped me realise that I was not alone in feeling this way and that, I was a natural giver. I learned how I could change my life, from a person who does everything for everyone else - to my own detriment - to a successful, happy individual that chooses to give to others in a resourceful and sustainable way.

This realisation and change didn't magically happen overnight but was a journey of self-discovery over a couple of years. But what I did overnight, was to decide to create a change in my life. Once I made that decision, my life completely changed in an instant.

Help Given, Never Accepted

There is great awareness around what "self-sabotage" is now and it has become the buzz phrase of today's society. According to yourdictionary.com, self-sabotage means "to sabotage oneself or one's plans. In other words, self-sabotage is when you follow a pattern or behaviour that will destroy the results you're actually looking for."

By constantly rescuing others, I was truly self-sabotaging myself because everything I was doing was to feel needed. I relied on others to make me happy.

My behaviour was focused on doing everything for everyone else to make them happy, to like and accept me.

But here's the thing – I was waiting for them to do the same thing for me.

Unfortunately, that would rarely occur. When it did occur, I would never accept it because it's my job to give to others, not to accept things from others. I didn't want to receive help from anyone because I was the one who helped others, not the other way around.

Enter the self-sabotage – as I was constantly focusing on everyone else's needs and how to make them happy.

This meant that *I never had to focus on me* and what made me happy.

In addition to that, I never had to take any kind of responsibility for my actions because I never did anything for myself, I only did things for everyone else.

I lived vicariously through others, by controlling their lives and their universe, instead of looking in my own back yard. Many of us do this and we spend so much time and energy trying to show others how to live their lives.

We are trying to help them because we love them, right? That's the reason we're constantly helping them, isn't it? Unfortunately, this is just not true. The real reason we rescue them, and my biggest learning, is because we want them to say, "You're right, Kleo!"

Because above all, I wanted them to like me. I wasn't doing it for them at all, I was doing it for me. In other words, I wanted to feel validated and important. Pretty selfish, isn't it? And we all do it.

Effectively we are trying to force people to do things they don't want to do, based on our standards, expectations, our beliefs and our values!

How dare we? How purely selfish and controlling can we get?

Expectations

> *"Expectation is the root of all heartache."*
> – William Shakespeare

Expectations can be your worst enemy. Because of the premise that we believe everyone else is exactly the same as us, for example, react the same way, treat people the same way, joke the same way, know what we're thinking, have the same standards and values as we do. But they don't!

And because of this assumption, we are constantly left feeling disappointed and let down.

The expectations that we place on others are extraordinarily high because we assume others should act and behave in the same ways we do. As we put so much effort into helping everyone else, we give a lot of ourselves to others without them ever asking for it. We naturally expect everyone else to do exactly the same thing in return. But they can't and it's not their fault!

Because we have to be the constant giver, servant and rescuer for our external approval, no one could ever give us back any kind of service or help because we would never allow them to.

This is why we have issues with accepting compliments, gifts or help from others. Because to us, it means that we are weak and we always have to be strong and always have to know what to do. We always have to know how to look after everyone and always have to be in "control" of any situation. We know what's best.

We constantly kill ourselves to forcibly control every single situation. But control is an illusion. What I mean is, you will never, ever be able to control anything or anyone and it's a false sense of reality that we ourselves have created.

Trying to control something is like trying to stop the ocean from breaking its waves on the shore of sand. There is no chance that you will ever be able to control this, so stop trying to. We constantly try to control everything because it makes us feel secure, safe and certain in our lives. The truth is you cannot ever control anything or anyone.

You try to control everything, which means that everything must always be done to the best of your ability and no one else will ever have a say in it. So how could anyone ever reach your expectations? They never will and they never can because your expectations of everyone else are so ridiculously high that no one will ever be able to meet them!

Not even you can meet your expectations!

The Moral

You can't help anyone that doesn't want help. Period! When a friend comes to you with a problem, instead of rescuing them, just shut up and actually listen to what they have to say. They might not even want your help, they may have never even asked for your help, they may just want to vent. So, shut up and listen!

Instead of trying to solve their "problem", ask them, "Do you want my help with this issue, or do you feel better just talking about it?"

Most of the time they say, "I just want to vent, because I've got this, I'm good."

More often than not they just want someone to listen. Sometimes it helps just to verbalise the problem because it enables them to have clarity on their issue. When this occurs, the true magic happens because they actually solve the problem for themselves right in front of you.

And you just Resourcefully Rescued a friend, just by shutting up and listening without judgment.

Remember, if you're jumping in and helping everyone then you're preventing them from actually learning the skills they need to learn to solve their own problems for themselves. In essence, we are preventing them from becoming a responsible and self-functioning adult.

Resourceful Rescuing

All of this information is to help you to move forward, but I can't control how you will use this, who you will tell or what your future actions will be. To give to others sustainably and resourcefully, you must first give to yourself.

Think of the Golden Goose from the children's story *Jack and the Beanstalk* published by Benjamin Tabart. Jack climbed the beanstalk to seek great treasures and found the Golden Goose, which he stole from the Giant and kept for himself. He basked in wealth and handed out the Golden Goose's golden eggs to everyone in the village.

Most of us know that this is where the story ends, in fact the Golden Goose died because in Jack's absentmindedness, he forgot to feed the Goose any food.

We do exactly the same thing to ourselves. We forget to feed and sustain ourselves first, before we absentmindedly rescue everyone around us.

So, if you're handing out the eggs, so to speak, you need to stop immediately because you're not actually putting any food in your Goose's mouth. How then can you continually make more eggs? But if you feed your Goose, take your time to nourish it with the right food and nutrition – then the world can be your Golden Egg.

How would you prefer to be? What would you prefer to do? What would you prefer to have? Would you prefer to bend over backwards absolutely killing yourself? Or would you prefer to give from a cup that's absolutely full and overflowing? The choice is always yours.

Now there are a couple of identifiers: If you're giving too much, you will start to feel tired, stretched, thin, weak, down and sleepy all the time. When you practice this resourcefully, you will feel energised, powerful, strong, revitalised, happy, peaceful, calm and relaxed every day.

Ripples

People will notice a difference in you, and it may take time for you to adjust. The most important part is to break the cycle.

Do whatever it takes to stop yourself from being the first person to put their hand up and learn the importance of saying no! After all, you don't always have to be the one to help.

This can cause some disruption within your family and relationships because everyone is so used to being rescued! You've been doing everything for them, so by taking a step back, you are forcing them to take a step forward. They may not like it at the start because it's different, it's unusual and it's not something that they're used to. But it is for their benefit, challenge and growth – they may not see it yet, but I promise that one day they will thank you for it.

Make sure that you stick to your guns, because you are worth it. You do deserve to be happy.

The best advice I can give you is to keep creating more of what you want in your life, regardless of others. Some of your friends may not want to be friends anymore. And they're only friends with you because you do everything for them and you were rescuing them. Ask yourself: do you want to be associated with those kinds of friends anyway?

You want to have friends and relationships that are resourceful. Give yourself an opportunity to hang out with different people that are resourceful and actually uplift you instead of dragging you down.

I now realise how happy I have become because I stopped trying to control everyone else's lives and started sustaining my own life. With the relationships in my life, I don't control what they do and I don't solve their problems. I let them come up with their own solutions.

I do however help them to see and identify the problem. When they want my help, I ask them, "What do you want to do about it?" I wait and let them come up with their own solution. When they do come up with a solution, I ask some additional questions, "Do you think that's going to work? Is this the best way forward for you?" Most of the time they reply, "Well, I could give it a shot and see what happens." Great, rock on and try that. If it doesn't work, then try something different.

This method has created a positive ripple effect through my family. It's allowing my kids to think for themselves and come up with their own solutions to their own problems. This will help them in the long run, especially when they grow up and become adults. They'll have the ability to solve their own problems and stand on their own two feet.

As you can see Resourceful Rescuing may sound challenging but in reality, it is really easy to do. The key to remember is to know your boundaries, know what you will allow in your life and what you will not allow in your life. Make time to do things that you want without dedicating all your time to helping everyone else.

> *"Use your time to create the choices you want in your life."*
> *– Kleo Merrick*

Enjoy,

Kleo Merrick

About the Author

Kleo Merrick is a #1 International Bestselling Author, Speaker, Online Course Strategist and adviser to Entrepreneurs and Small Business Owners.

Kleo is the CEO of Merrick Courses, a company she founded in 2013 where she runs successful Workshops, Online Training Programs and also teaches businesses on how to increase profits, leveraging their skills and knowledge by creating Online Courses.

She is the author of *Compelling Selling: How To Earn More By Selling Less* and *Yes I Can: 16 Success Secrets from Inspiring People Around The World.*

Kleo has created multiple Online Courses and Programs, such as her signature *Online Warrior 5-Day Free Training*, teaching individuals how to convert their skills and knowledge into Online Courses and Programs that they can Sell and Make Money While They Sleep.

Kleo is extremely passionate about helping entrepreneurs and business owners fulfil their potential and share their truth with the world.

Merrick Courses Pty Ltd

Website: www.kleomerrick.com
Email: kleo@kleomerrick.com
Facebook: https://www.facebook.com/kleomerrickpage/
Instagram: https://www.instagram.com/kleomerrick/
LinkedIn: https://www.linkedin.com/in/kleomerrick/

Dedication

To my fellow unresourceful rescuers, you have the power within you to let go, take charge of your own life and with that … control your destiny.

Chapter Four

Your LIFE, Your CHOICE!
by Joslyn A Gardiner
Author, Speaker, Retreat and Workshop Facilitator, Australia

"Your external world is a direct reflection of your internal values."
– Joslyn Gardiner

The Fantasy

I was born in Wanganui, just north of Wellington on the North Island of New Zealand, the second eldest of five children. My parents had grown up in the area and, as top athletes, were well known. Our family was privileged. My grandfather was president of *the club*, and highly regarded in New Zealand rugby. Dad excelled at rugby. We were welcomed everywhere.

Looking back, I can clearly see the events that instilled my beliefs and values, as well as the determination and focus, which drove me to persevere and create the success I have enjoyed in business. I started my first business at eight years old selling white mice. Highly profitable and I was hooked!

My upbringing taught me resilience, honesty, money management and adaptability but most of all: How you live is up to you – It's Your Choice!

My passion has always been travelling. Between leaving New Zealand and moving to Australia, I spent 25 years living in Fiji, Solomon Islands and South Africa, amazing experiences I highly recommend. In Fiji and Solomon Islands, my life was filled with "what other people paid money to do!" I even picked up my soulmate, Steve.

So, skip forward to the present and I am living a truly blessed life. Steve and I have worked together for 15 years in our hypnotherapy business. Steve works with clients to overcome addictive behaviours, long-term anxiety, stress and post-traumatic-stress-disorder. I facilitate online courses, workshops and educational retreats for businesswomen to Relax, Realign and Reset their lives. It's a far cry from where I started!

My childhood was typically dysfunctional but still alright … until it wasn't!

The first ten years of my life, I recall as being "special" or privileged.

Sport was a big focus for my father. We were expected to follow in his footsteps. For me this was easy as I loved the discipline and competition. Unfortunately, my brother and sisters did not share my father's passion for sport and this created a huge tension in the family. My father wanted us to achieve the "greatness" he didn't.

Dad did not know how to win or lose gracefully, but he made it his business to teach us this skill. Every time we won, we moved up a grade. I became good at being second. Lots of lessons – good and bad – were learnt through this, and never being good enough was the one that stuck with me!

Sport was my escape. I could be *me,* an individual with achievements of my own. I used sport to be seen, to get the recognition from my parents I desperately craved. At home, I was the odd one out. A member of the family but not part of it. An intruder who could not speak about success, and any failure was met with scorn. Luckily, I found mentors in the sporting world who encouraged, advised and praised me.

Reality Hits

When I was eleven years old, my world fell apart. I do not know what happened. We moved away from everything and everyone I loved. In Wanganui I was surrounded by aunts, uncles and dozens of cousins. They were my role models. We left everyone behind and moved to Tokoroa. It was only 400 kilometres away but ten hours by bus made it seem like the end of the earth.

Tokoroa. I hated it. I hated everything and everyone. Most of all, I hated the change in our circumstances.

Wanganui equalled big house, family, privilege and familiarity. Tokoroa was a tiny house – five kids in a one-bedroom house. Three of us slept in an annexe. My parents and the two little ones in the bedroom. The ugly blue house. I hated it. I hated the way the neighbours treated us.

"White trash" I was called the first day at my new school. My parents fought. We had no money. We had no friends. I was devastated. My parents were in survival mode, as were the rest of my siblings. I learnt quickly that if it was going to be, it was up to me if I wanted anything to change.

I decided sport would be my ticket in. The obvious choice was softball. I had played competitively in Wanganui so I knew I could hold my own. I was wrong! I was so badly bullied that I left the team within weeks. Netball was the same. I was the out-of-town kid that no one wanted around. I was too short for volleyball or basketball. I couldn't play tennis to save myself.

Fortunately, none of the bullies wanted to play badminton. At last I had an outlet for my frustration, my anger and an opportunity to become accepted in this new community. Luckily, I was good at it.

On the surface, life appeared better. I was still trying to belong, to feel accepted, but I struggled. At home I was the odd one out. I thought differently. I wanted more! There had to be more.

The truth was I was looking for the past. I was looking for someone to guide me. I knew that was all I needed. Someone! I found another mentor.

The First "What The ..."

I left school at fourteen. Not really left; I just didn't go back. My holiday job was offered with a four-year internship, I accepted it in a heartbeat. I could see the potential of this career.

My teachers were horrified. What was I thinking? *Finish high school! You will regret it.* But I thought I knew what I wanted. I had seen life with choices and without choices. To choose, you need money. My job gave me choices and mentors. People who had what I wanted.

I loved my job and progressed quickly. I had control. I was always good with money. My wage wasn't much but I divided it into three. A third would be to save, for board and for bills – I still do this to this day.

Life was good.

I Bought the Dream

In the seventies, girls were sold "the Dream". Find a guy, get married, buy a house, have kids ... life will be great!

I bought the Dream.

I met "my guy". Within twelve months we were married. At twenty years old, I had three children. I gave up what I wanted and accepted *what was expected*.

What the Hell Was I Thinking?

Twenty years old, no qualifications, no work experience, three children and a totally dysfunctional marriage. My Dream had become a nightmare. A nightmare of my own making and one I was told to live with. *You made your bed, now lie in it!*

I knew **it was up to me**, it was my choice to live differently.

It was difficult. The verbal abuse was relentless. A persecutor never needs to lift a hand if they know the right words to hurt you. The belief that I wasn't good enough, I wasn't smart enough, or who did I think I was kept me locked into a life I hated. I had to get out!

To change my circumstances, I needed education, qualifications and the guts to leave.

I went back to school. To be accepted into university I had to complete high school. So, I did. Yes, my teachers were right. This was the hard way, but it was the only way. It was embarrassing to sit exams in a classroom with seventeen-year-olds.

I was accepted into university and studied Business Management. It took six years of studying by correspondence (before computers) to qualify. Was it hard? Yes. Did I feel like giving up? Never! My greatest fear was that I would fail. I was so terrified that I wasn't good enough to pass the exams.

My Life Was Chaotic

I got a job – I worked full time; looked after my children and studied. They say if you want something done, ask a busy person to do it! How true is that? I was frantically busy!

I studied every free moment: at night and during my lunch breaks. My days started at 4.30am. I slept listening to tapes of lectures held weeks earlier in Australia. I typed assignments on a portable typewriter. My deadlines were confirmed by Post Office date stamps and secured by flights back to Australia. I think back to that crazy time of "bribing" post office workers to add one more item to the already sealed post bag.

Then I got lucky! I found a mentor!

Life was crazy. I kept the goal in mind. I had to qualify. I needed my financial independence. Finally, the last exam. The final pass. I qualified. It was up to me. I did it. I got my freedom. The freedom to choose my life.

Rebuilding My Life

During the years of study, my marriage disintegrated, and we separated. Emotionally, I was wrecked. I found two ways to deal with this: sport and mentors.

I needed a way to release my pent-up emotions – frustration, anger and hurt – that was threatening to bubble over at work. Sport had always been my escape, and squash and scuba diving came to my rescue. Playing squash against twenty-year-old males, taught me valuable lessons every woman needs to know to compete in a male-dominated business world. One, have a strategy and a plan. Two, don't back down to bullying.

My job had an unusual component to it. As an Accountant Manager for an international company, one of my duties was to play golf with visitors. Golf was a passion of mine, so I was happy to play golf every Wednesday, and I didn't mind getting paid to do it.

The biggest benefit was being "forced" to communicate and socialise with people every week. I met successful businesspeople, politicians and sports personalities from across the globe. I asked questions, sought advice, listened to how, what and why people were successful in sport, business and politics. I learnt that success is never by accident, it is always by design! I found mentors in the strangest places, all of whom freely shared their pearls of wisdom on business and success.

Step by Step I Rebuilt My Life

Achieving my goal to be financially independent instilled confidence in my ability to succeed.

One of my mentors in Honiara was a good friend, Steve. My diving buddy adjudicated my exams and proofread my assignments. Oftentimes, I hated him for his *red pen corrections* but his guidance and support got me through whenever my self-belief wavered. When my contract ended in Honiara, I had nowhere to go and being a divorcee did not leave me with many friends or choices.

Who Does That?

Steve had returned home to Southern Africa. A quick phone call, and I packed up and moved across the world. Another "what the hell was I thinking" decision! Yes, I know, who does that? I admit, I didn't think it through. Who packs up their life into two suitcases, kids in tow and moves to South Africa, where racial tension, carjackings and murders happen daily? No, I didn't think it through. It was simply the only place I had a friend. It was the best decision I ever made for myself, for my children, and for my future.

Accidental Business Success

In South Africa, you learn to adapt. You must, in order to survive.

After five years, I brought a "sort of" franchise. Within three months I recovered my costs and tripled my investment. However, the product changed frequently! Greeting cards, oil paintings, security alarms, timeshare. I adapted each time. I made money but I didn't like the model!

So, I opened my own business, Panda, a "Robin Hood" concept that grew to a quarter-million-dollar business in five years. We supplied educational products into African townships – another story, another time! I look back on this time in townships and wonder "what the hell was I thinking" but it was the most satisfying years of my life.

Things Change

In 1996, we moved to Australia. Broke again, we worked our backsides off. Then Steve was made redundant! We had just bought a house, our daughter and family living with us. I made the irrational decision to resign from my high-paying full-time job and accept a part-time contract position! It set us up for life! The best "what the hell" decision ever! I was working for a personal development company and Steve and I became coaches!

What I Learned Along the Way

Life is not the "survival of the fittest" but for those who can change and adapt.

There are so many "what the hell was I thinking" moments in my life. I wondered what drove them. I later found out when Dr John Demartini introduced me to "values", the true driving force within us all.

Every decision I made was to fulfill a value – a void in my life I needed to fill.

Living the Dream

Steve and I built our business on a foundation of values. We value recognition, contribution, creating wealth and education. We wanted a six-figure income, and our plan from Day 1 was to achieve this. In the beginning, we struggled. We were broke! However, we found a mentor, then another, while focusing on one thing, and success followed.

Our business, Transformations, was recognised for innovation and expertise as Queensland finalist in the Telstra Small Business Awards. That party was a night of "ticking off" values!

In 2016, 2017 and 2018, we were finalists in the Redlands City Business Awards.

My first goal was financial independence. The second lifestyle. I had achieved both.

Words of Wisdom

Overcoming my "unconscious beliefs" allowed me to go back to school, build two successful businesses (and now a third) and travel the world.

All my life mentors have appeared when I needed them. Mentors come in all guises! It is said, "When the student is ready, the teacher appears." This has been true for me.

Here are some of the "pearls of wisdom" I live by.

- **Your Life Is Your Choice.** You have the power to change anything in your life. It may be hard, take time or seem impossible, but you decide and it's done!
- **Trust Your Gut** – It's your subconscious mind talking to you
- **Mentors**. Ask people to mentor you. Hire a coach. These are three who helped me:
    - Aunt Myrtle
    - » **Save a third of everything you earn. Always have a Plan B.**
    - My Sports coach
    - » **You only fail when you give up.**
    - » **The only opinion that matters is yours. You know if you did your best!**
    - Benjamin J Harvey
    - » **Focus on one thing until you are an expert.**
- Business Building Tips
    - Build your business the right way, from the beginning.
    - Have a business plan.
    - Set your vision, aligned with your values.
    - Focus on one thing until you earn recognition.

- Pay yourself first.
- Ensure you are dispensable.
- Have an Exit Plan.

Finally...

My best decisions were made when I went with my Gut – those "what the hell was I thinking" moments brought me the blessed lifestyle I live today!

Do I regret them? Hell no! In the end, we only regret the chances we didn't take! So take risks!

My Motto

*"Follow the three Rs
Respect for Others, Respect for Self, Responsibility for Your Actions
Never, Never Give Up."*

Wishing you success,

Joslyn Gardiner

About the Author

Joslyn Gardiner is a speaker, workshop and retreat facilitator and business mentor.

Joslyn and her husband Steve founded Transformations Coaching & Hypnotherapy in 2006.

Over the past 20 years, Joslyn has studied human behaviour and specialises in running successful workshops and online personal development programmes. Joslyn's programmes focus on eliminating negative Unconscious Core Beliefs and aligning Your Why with your Values.

Joslyn loves teaching people how to set up and grow micro-businesses into profitable companies. Her speciality is removing the mind blocks preventing business owners from "charging" a fair price for their services.

In 2019, Joslyn launched her latest venture: Life Change Retreats – designed specifically to enable women in business to take time out to Reset, Recharge, Refocus!

Transformations Coaching and Hypnotherapy

Life Change Retreats: Seven days of adventure, laughter, learning to re-align with your Values

Online Courses:

- **Transform Your Life** – Align Your Why, What Goals With Values
- **Your Values Reflect Your Reality** – Learn what really drives your decision, choices and outcomes.
- **Making Money Matter** – Money flows to where it is most managed. Learn to manage your money to grow wealth easily

Workshops: More details on our website.

Website: https://www.transformyou.com.au/

Email: joslyn@transformyou.com.au

Facebook: https://www.facebook.com/JoslynGardiner/

Instagram: https://www.instagram.com/joslyngardiner

LinkedIn: https://www.linkedin.com/in/joslyn-ann-gardiner/

YouTube: https://www.youtube.com/user/LifeArchitects

Skype: Sys4Success

Dedication

With thanks to Steve, who saved me from myself, my doubts and fears and gave me the freedom to become who I am today!

Chapter Five

Rejection Can't Kill You
by Scott Lawrence
Clinical Hypnotherapist, Speaker and Author, Australia

"I don't care if you're smart, show me your heart."
– *Scott Lawrence*

In 2009, I had just graduated from the Academy of Hypnotic Science. My dream was to learn hypnotherapy and then to base a career around it. One of my fellow students invited me to his 50th birthday, and as we drank a beer together, he told me that he bought the Academy.

This was great news for me because I could join up as a lecturer. I loved what I was taught so much that I could just about recite it all word for word. So I asked the new owner of the Academy of Hypnotic Science if I could get on board as a lecturer and to help him to build the academy.

It took courage to ask, but I'm glad that I did.

Unfortunately, the answer was "No".

Not only was the answer a "No", but it was one of those noes that come with feedback. They told me that all I had was a diploma in hypnotherapy and no experience in the field. I didn't have any training qualifications and had nothing to bring to the table. I hadn't proven myself in any way and they've already been asked by quite a few academy graduates if they can teach.

Of course, it looks attractive to a graduate to get paid $400 per day to teach their favourite topic for five hours per day and then go home risk free. It's a dream. But that dream needed to get backed up with a TAE, training and assessment certificate and industry experience. I didn't have either, so I was completely crushed. I felt as though my last two years of training now meant nothing.

As a kid, the third and last born, I was often ignored. Don't get me wrong, I always had a roof over my head and food to eat. I grew up with a not-so-rare, yet expensive skin condition. It was nothing life threatening, but both of my parents had to work to pay for my medication. Basically, it meant that my older brother and sister got to spend time with my parents as they were growing up, but when I was born, I missed out and was ignored.

My dad once said to a friend jokingly, "You teach everything you know to your youngest kid." I found it hard to learn anything in school because I just didn't get any support. I wasn't popular in school and even the teachers used to bully me. I became such an introvert.

I was willing to do anything to just gain some life skills and to just find my place in the world. It was a lonely journey, but as soon as I finished high school, I found any job that would teach me something. I did managerial roles and then finally in my mid-20s, I signed up to study hypnotherapy. I was curious to know about hypnotherapy because I felt that it would lead to answers about my life and why I was the way that I was. And it was amazing. I learned social skills and self-reflection that I had never heard about or had any access to previously. Hypnotherapy was a life saver. I became addicted.

My favourite life lesson is that my life values will get me through any situation. This sounds like an oversimplification, but let me explain.

As a kid, youngest of three, when I was presented with a problem, I didn't know how to fix it. If I got bullied, I would freeze like a deer in the headlights. If I got asked a question by my teachers, I'd freeze like a deer in the headlights. Basically, I did a lot of freezing like a deer in the headlights.

After I started to study psychology, I was able to swap "Deer in the headlights" for a few new techniques. If somebody asked me a question, I'd lean on one of my values of "Have a go and see what happens", so I'd have a go at answering their question.

If I needed money, I leant of the value of "Activity creates income" and I had a go at doing some advertising and attracted clients.

If I didn't know how to do something, I leant on the value of "Ask somebody who knows best" and then I would call an expert or study a course until I knew the answer.

But what do you do when you don't know enough? Again, as a kid, I didn't know any values to get me through situations, except for one.

The only value that I knew as a child was, "Hang in there, it may get better someday."

The reason why I put so much emphasis on "Values will get you through any situation" is because before I learned what my values were, I basically wasn't getting through. I was simply suffering.

I grew up with Aspergers (AS). It's not deadly, but it does stunt your social growth, especially when you're the youngest of 3 and mostly ignored. When I saw the other kids having fun, socialising and just being normal, I didn't know how to join in.

It's like showing up to a war where everybody has full body armour, guns and driving a tank, and you turn up wearing thongs (flip flops if you're American) and a t-shirt and don't even know that there is a war going on.

There was this girl that I was very interested in when I started high school. A normal guy would have just asked her out. But not me.

She even asked me one time if she could sit next to me.

How did I respond?

I froze like a "Deer in the Headlights".

That must have been weird for her. She asked me a question and put herself out there and I just creeped her out by just staring back blankly like a "Deer in the Headlights".

It was very uncomfortable for both of us, I assure you.

I spent years regretting freezing up like that.

It was like something was missing from my brain, but somehow, every other person out there seemed to know what to do.

One of my favourite values that has gotten me through life is "Rejection can't kill you".

After I studied hypnotherapy, I had a toolbox of values. One of my first moves was to get back into the dating game after being single for five years. So, I asked out a girl who I later married. Yes, that marriage didn't last, but "Rejection can't kill you". This is an important value to know about. My all-time favourite value is "People don't care what's on your mind. They care what's on your heart."

As I started to let my guard down, ask people for what I wanted, not feeling rejection and telling people who I felt, I started to receive more rewards in the Money and Love departments of life.

I asked again to become a lecturer at the Academy of Hypnotic Science and told the owner about how I feel about the industry, and I became the highest paid lecturer there.

I asked people to buy my programmes/courses, I asked for space at home, I asked for company, lowered my filters and told people what was on my heart.

Another value that's made so much sense is that "Nobody gets there alone". It's tempting to avoid asking for help, but avoiding doesn't make us look stronger in the eyes of everybody else for handling everything alone. Most people can see through a macho act.

It takes courage to ask, but "Rejection Can't Kill You".

I asked the universe for a mentor who was close enough to my age that I felt that I could relate to them. So the universe sent me Ryan.

Ryan, at only age 24, had already built a social media company that he grew to over $10,000,000 per year.

I got to travel the world with Ryan, from Melbourne, Sydney, Switzerland, Hawaii and we'd sit next to each other on the planes just talking about life and business.

His ultimate advice for me was to learn how to do phone sales. He said, "If you'd just pick up the phone, your business would triple."

It was uncomfortable because phone sales have this real Icky feeling. People can be rude to you. And even if you go in with noble intentions, you can still get hung up on.

After a while, I picked up the skill and found that if you're strong and confident, they stop testing you with their nonsense and they start to really listen to what you have to say. I stopped trying to be a people pleaser and just got to the point more quickly.

The real change for me is that I no longer have to live my life in frustration because I lean on my values.

I move quickly and I do what I want, because my experience has let me know how to make the best of a situation. I would never have been able to do this if I wasn't trained.

It may have actually been a benefit to me that I started off in life frustrated to the point where I put education first, because I see so many people live their entire lives frustrated because they won't ask for help or get a coach. Sometimes falling apart is a blessing because it actually makes you cross a boundary that you would have spent your whole life inside of.

I am now free. I am loved and I am happier than I've been in the past. I value these things now. I value my freedom, being loved and being happy. You need to value these things too if you're going to get anywhere.

Get as much education as you can, allow the education to shape your values and let those values guide your life.

Ask for help, act quickly, don't take advice from somebody who is afraid of life and let your natural genius flow.

Honestly, I don't have to stress too hard about anything because I've learned how to create what I want stress free.

Is your mind holding you back, stressing out or are you suffering? It doesn't have to be this way.

If you want to grow your business, there are three core areas that you should focus on.

1. Get High Quality Leads as Cheaply as Possible
2. Give Away Training in Videos and eBooks to your Leads
3. Create an Email Sequence that sells for you or Learn to Sell on the phone. Both skills can be Learned when you talk to the Right People.

To get you started, I want to give you my eBook, *How to Get Your 6 Figure Funnel Finished in 3 Weeks*, for free:

- http://therapistfunnels.com/Lawrence_Hypnotherapy/6FigeBook/6FigeBook.html

Download it, read it and email me to let me know what you learned, are putting into action and what results you're getting.

Also, you'll need to know how to create Facebook Videos that Attract Thousands of Dollars.

Grab my eBook here:

- http://therapistfunnels.com/Lawrence_Hypnotherapy/Facebook_Video_Ebook/Attract_Hypnotherapy_Clients_eBook.html

Again, one of my favourite values is that I like to do things quickly and I don't like to muck around when I have a project to do. I also like people who share that same value.

If you share that same value, then email me to let me know what you're working on.

Again, it's been a pleasure, and thank you so much for reading.

Stay Safe, but not afraid, and live life by your values, not by somebody else's. Thank you again.

> *"If you wait for life to bring you what you want, you'll be waiting forever."*
> – Scott Lawrence

Thank you again,

About the Author

Scott Lawrence is Clinical Hypnotherapist and Marketing Coach.

Scott is the Founder of Social Media Mastery, created in 2019, running Online Classes, Live Workshops and Training Books on the art of Growing Your Social Media Empire Online.

His clients say: "The hand holding that Scott gives you is Gold. I needed a coach that actually answers my questions fast so that I can get on with it."

He is the author of How to Cure the Anxiety Loop and 4 Hour Course and has created the following programmes:

- "How to Hypnotise an Addict" – An Online Class to teach foundational therapy skills to people who work with addiction.
- "Business in a Box" – A 3-Week Online Crash Course in business to show you the strategies that millionaires use to earn over $20,000 per week.
- "7 Figure Asset" – A 12-Month Training Program to get you to complete the entire business, from marketing, product delivery and market share.
- "7 Figure Funnel" – A 3-Week Online Program that gives you the Exact Steps to turn your "How to" business into an Empire.

Scott is a Straight Talker who has the Skill to Make Everything Simple.

Lawrence Hypnotherapy

Website: http://therapistfunnels.com/Lawrence_Hypnotherapy/50_Leads/50_Free_Leads.html
Email: scott@lawrencehypnotherapy.com
Facebook: https://www.facebook.com/scott.lawrence.5099

Dedication

To my family for supporting me and believing in me. And to my students all around the world who inspire me with their passions and dedication to creating a world of empowerment for all to see.

Chapter Six

Navigating the Waves
by Kitiboni Rolle Adderley
Physiotherapist and Certified Health Coach, Nassau, Bahamas

"Life will send you a series of waves. These waves can overwhelm you at times, but you have the choice to become submerged, swim or surf the waves."
– Kitiboni Rolle Adderley

Craft Your Story

If you're reading this, this is my third book project. I never dreamed that I would ever be an author, much less co-author and published in three books in one year. This year got off to a rocky start and by the third month, we knew that this year would be very different.

2020 has proven to be a year of upheaval to life as we knew it. We could not have prepared for the lockdowns, curfews, stalled economies, restricted travel and enforced personal protection safety laws. It seems that our world had shifted overnight. The reality is that it will never shift back to life as we knew it – to what was our normal.

As my business slowed to a trickle, I found myself doing like many others worldwide, pivoting and looking for alternate means of income. I moved the majority of my physical therapy care online, to what we refer to as telehealth or telerehabilitation. It was one of the best decisions. It also came with a bonus.

I began to pull on my health and life coaching skills to help patients and clients. Many were experiencing difficulties adjusting to the changes that the COVID-19 pandemic brought and needed more than physical therapy intervention. They reported that they felt overwhelmed, isolated and one client used the word drowning. I knew they needed coping skills. These were skills that I was equipped with. I never dreamt that I would be serving women in this capacity as an online coach.

In the past, my friends would often call me, and asked me for advice and suggestions. Like a good friend I would sit down and listen. I would offer the advice and suggestions that I thought were appropriate to help my girlfriend succeed. I also had this experience with some of my male friends. Whether it was advice on health, relationships or careers, we seem to be able to sit down and fashion a plan or approach to getting things done.

Here, I was now doing it as a business service. I am helping people navigate the waves during these turbulent times. Providing support and motivation when they feel like they need help staying buoyant. I am providing them tools to improve their competence as they swim towards their goals. It is so rewarding to see their confidence increase and they surf through successfully. I did it!

A Glimpse Into My World

I am the eldest of three in the Union of my parents. From early on, my dad instilled a keen sense of responsibility in me. As the oldest sibling, it was imperative that I kept the younger children in line and ensured that they carried out the tasks and chores that had been set for them. When the younger two did not complete their tasks, I was punished for it. I learned how to take care and assist others incredibly early from this. This is perhaps where I also developed the habits of being a nurturer and also feeling that it is my responsibility to ensure that everyone and everything is okay.

I have been a physical therapist since 2000. I started my career in the hospital setting. It was a fantastic opportunity for education, growth, networking and community building. I love learning, so being surrounded by multidisciplinary teams afforded me access to information skills and perspectives on a regular basis. My confidence as a young physical therapist also grew. I have never been afraid to ask questions when it came to learning about the profession. I knew at the time that I needed as much moulding and guidance as I could possibly get being a new professional. I absolutely love learning.

For the last sixteen years, I have been a private practice owner. Handling Your Health Wellness & Rehab is a wellness and physiotherapy clinic dedicated to providing holistic and integrative approach to rehabilitation and health coaching. We have done well over the years, building a strong following and loyal customer base. There are families where we treat three generations.

The Drama

I decided that the time was right for me to pursue my Doctorate in Physiotherapy. I figured it was now or never. The truth is, I should have enrolled in the Doctor of Physical Therapy Program in 2006. I had all my applications filled out and documents and references ready to go. Then I got pregnant. I parked the idea of obtaining my Doctorate and turned my focus on raising my new baby and caring for my family. Four years later I welcomed my third daughter. You can say that both of my hands were full.

I was still running my physical therapy clinic full-time and now taking care of three children. I knew I was unable to commit to a doctorate programme at that time, so I pursued short courses and certifications to keep myself current and increase my skill set and hence increase the service offering at the clinic.

I focused strongly on oncology/cancer rehabilitation related courses. Cancer rehabilitation is truly one of my passions. One of the certifications I received during this time was a Certified Health Coach for Institute of Integrative Nutrition. This was one of the best courses that I have invested in. It armed me with skills to have a more holistic approach to my patients and client's care.

In 2016, being married for ten years, I figured now was the time for me to go after this Doctorate in Physical Therapy. The American Physical Therapy Association had created a Vision 2020, where all physical therapists in the USA should obtain a Doctorate. I was determined that I would be a part of that vision.

I gathered all my applications and documents together yet again, but this time sent them off to the institution. When I got the acceptance email from Utica College for their Doctor of Physical Therapy Program, I was ecstatic. I had prepared to ride this wave for more than 12 years and finally, the opportunity was here. I was so excited.

My orientation was scheduled in Sarasota, Florida, for the 7th of January 2016 – my Uncle Lionel died just four days before that. OMG! He was just 48 years old. He had been admitted to the hospital a few weeks earlier due to a stroke. Although the stroke was severe. I had envisioned him being discharged from the hospital and I would give him intensive physical therapy for stroke rehabilitation to get him back as close to his old self again. We were robbed of that opportunity. He was not supposed to die!

You need to understand the magnitude of my loss. This man was not just my uncle. Although he was my father's younger brother, there were only eight years between us. He was my big brother and my alternate dad, my confidante and coach, my diary, my Kleenex and teddy bear, my chef and my comedian. He was such a massive part of my life. He was the master of ceremony at my wedding. He called me Dr Kiti from the time I graduated with my first degree in 2000. He said, "I know that you will be our doctor."

Uncle Lionel's death left a void that I do not think could ever be filled. His death knocked the wind out of me. I sank beneath the waves. If it wasn't for the fact that I had invested thousands of dollars in tuition, had already purchased the plane ticket, booked the hotel room and rental car, I would not have made it.

I bawled as I made my way through the airport. I bawled as I drove myself across the Sunshine Skyway Bridge leaving Tampa for Sarasota. I sat in the Orientation and bawled. I was a mess – awashed in tears, but I was there, I showed up. I had to do it. I had to get this done for Lionel, so I could finally be the Dr Kiti he knew I could be.

The Inner Struggle

Here is where I really felt submerged. It was like I truly was drowning here. I was drowning in work at the clinic and in my schoolwork. Although the Doctorate programme was primarily online, the work, research and assignments were intense. I was still trying to see a full patient load in the clinic, of course, because the bills still needed to be paid.

Caring for oncology/cancer patients can be quite physically, mentally and emotionally taxing. Cancer patients or survivors usually need more support and care than the average orthopaedic patient. The hands-on care and emotional investment can be intense, so at the end of the day, I am spent and running on fumes. Usually I need a few minutes to revive and I am good, but things were not happening like they should.

Through all this, my two younger princesses, now six and ten, had their homework, after school clubs, dance classes and birthday parties. This was a lot. I tried to be there for everything.

However, there were times when I was drowning in guilt. I was drowning in grief and all stages that come with grief; denial and isolation, anger, bargaining (with me and with loved ones), depression and acceptance. I was caught in an undertow of these emotions and stages – cycling through them daily.

I was struggling. I needed help. I didn't really know how to ask for help. I know that that sounds strange, however, it is true. I am so used to being independent and being the one who is always helping others that I find it difficult asking for help.

The other challenge for me when it comes to asking for help is that I have an expectation that others would treat me like I would treat them. I usually see the needs of my friends and loved ones and try to fill them. That is the big sister trait in me. I expect others to do the same for me, but that is rarely the case. That unmet expectation comes with a great deal of disappointment and I decide that I can do it by myself and yet again overextend myself.

You often expect your loved ones to share the excitement that you do, but that is not the case sometimes. I found that during this voyage, the person that I expected to be there the most, my husband at the time, seemed to be the least supportive. That was painful to accept. I was disappointed, hurt, afraid but I kept swimming and I did it anyway. I finished the course with a 3.0+ grade point average. I walked across the stage and was hooded and received my doctorate.

I accomplished my goal, but I felt battered, by the waves of the last eighteen months. I was exhausted from struggling through the surf. I was physically and mentally exhausted. I had been so focused on keeping everything afloat, the children, my marriage, work and my grades, that I blocked out so many emotions.

That, coupled with a deteriorating marriage, I felt myself sinking. I knew I had to seek help. I had been so busy trying to keep everyone and everything together, I had neglected my physical, emotional and mental. I helped everyone, and made sure that everyone was okay but I had grossly neglected myself.

Breakthrough

I needed to do what I had to do for me. No one was going to do it for me. I started a serious practice of self-love and self-care. I had to get me into shipshape again. I sought counselling. Getting professional help helped me process the emotional and mental baggage that I had stored away as distractions. If I was to move forward, it would be in my best interest to unpack these emotions and lighten the load.

The process was taxing and painful but it was one of the best things that I could have done. I had to unpack the grief and other emotions, name them and release them. I had to create the space to receive the good and positives. I had to acknowledge and accept that not everyone is made to come on this journey with us. I had to accept that my expectations were just that – expectations. That not all of our friends and loved ones share our enthusiasm about the fact that we want better.

Expectations can lead to big disappointments. If you think about it, we often let ourselves down. I had to ask forgiveness from my children and other family members and friends. I had to forgive myself. Doing these actions and getting a better understanding makes things clearer. There will be less waves for you to navigate.

The Present and Future

Because of my journey and the training I sought, I can help others navigate their own journey. "I Did It!" I want to help others get through it with support and coaching. Far too many of us suffer in silence. We suffer long and needlessly. My coaching session can help you:

- Get to know yourself better by understanding your strengths and weaknesses.
- Develop effortless and natural strategies to make desired changes quick and easy.
- Loosen limiting beliefs.
- Evaluate your emotional and behavioural state to achieve a balanced work-play ratio.
- Brainstorm solutions and provide strategies to overcome challenges and blocks.
- Learn to develop the motivation game and emanate positive difference in the lives of others.
- Point you towards your success destination and set the right outcomes and solutions.

Wisdom

You need to have the basic skill to "hold your breath" for periods of time – proper breathing technique is a must. You must learn how to stay buoyant and float – you don't have to react to everything, Sometimes, you just need to go with the flow. With these minimum skills at least, you will not drown.

Basic minimum skills are not enough if you are about to go and conquer goals. You need to have some directions and movement. Swimming through waves can be quite difficult and hard work. You need strength and stamina to stay the course. The more you swim the more you build stamina, so you must stay at it. You need to train.

Surfing requires a whole other level of skill and strength, you must swim out and meet the wave, mount your board while on the wave and stay balanced as you ride this wave out. You need to have a thorough understanding of what you are getting yourself into, the tools you need and the direction that you are going towards.

Ideally you want to sail with a crew but often, it will be you alone on that surfboard for the most part. The crew usually comes after you have done most of the groundwork.

Make sure you try and secure a good rescue team. A team of friends and family that stay close when you are out there by yourself. They should be close enough that they can reach out and grab you when you get tired or fall off for a bit. You should always have support.

Questions to ask yourself:

1. Am I seaworthy – am I equipped with the skills?
2. Do I understand the task at hand?
3. Is this the right wave at the right time?

> *"A smooth sea never made a skilled sailor."*
> *– Franklin D. Roosevelt*

Wishing you wellness,

Kitiboni ~

About the Author

Dr Kitiboni (Kiti) Rolle Adderley, DPT, is a physical therapist and a wellness and recovery expert in Nassau, Bahamas. She loves helping women who have been diagnosed with breast cancer, diabetes, fibromyalgia and other chronic diseases to stay active and continue doing the things that they love. Kiti believes that prevention is better than cure and that there must be a holistic approach to the patient and the community.

She has dedicated her time and knowledge educating the public about wellness and how to manage chronic non-communicable diseases such as diabetes and hypertension. She has launched her podcast *Recovering the Whole of You,* which highlights the work of medical and wellness professionals and educates the audience about health and wellness topics. Kiti is currently serving as the Chair of the North American and Caribbean Region of World Physiotherapy.

She has recently become a number one international best-selling author on Amazon with the collaborations *Yes I Can … 16 Success Secrets from Inspiring Women Around the World* and *Pendulum of a Mother's Love*.

Kiti enjoys spending time with her three daughters. She also enjoys immersing herself in nature, travelling and experiencing other cultures, reading, cooking and crafting.

Handling Your Health Wellness & Rehab

Book: Yes I Can … 16 Success Secrets from Inspiring Women Around the World (https://bit.ly/328HVpE)

Website: www.HYHwellness.com

Email: DrKitiboni@handlingyourhealth.com

Facebook: https://www.facebook.com/Dr-Kitiboni-Rolle-Adderley-Physical-Therapist-307034383446563/

Handling Your Health @ Home Facebook Group:
https://www.facebook.com/groups/283378102655658/

Instagram: https://www.instagram.com/handlingyourhealth/

LinkedIn: https://www.linkedin.com/in/kitiboniphysiotherapist/

Twitter: https://twitter.com/CaribbeanPhysio

Dedication

This is dedicated to Uncle Lionel Elliott II, the first man to ever call me Dr Kitiboni, and to all my sisters out there who are trying to gracefully navigate the waves of life while balancing self, family, and work. "I Did It," so can you! I see you. I know that you are trying hard.

Give yourself grace. Learn how to take big breaths, you need it for when you get submerged by the waves. Keep focused and stay strong so you can swim in the right direction through the waves. Stay balanced and grounded as you surf the waves, so you don't lose yourself and that you always remember why you started this journey in the first place. Enjoy the Ocean of Life.

Chapter Seven

The Joy of Finding Self-Confidence and Self-Esteem

by Carol Davies

Author, Speaker, Success Strategist Coach, Optimist, Podcaster

"Shoot for the stars. You are so very important. This changing world needs your ideas, skills, caring and love. Go out and succeed!"
– Carol Davies

It's All About Finding Your True Self

You hear a lot about getting clarity about yourself, your career and other aspects of your life. So, what is this buzzword "clarity" and why is it important to have in your life? Simply put, "clarity" is about getting clear about what is important in your life, what drives you to act and succeed. It has a lot to do with finding your purpose in life. Do you question your life path, passions, hopes and dreams?

Are you saying, "My life's not going where I want it to go, I must not be good enough, I want to give up." Or, "I know this is what I should be doing but I spend SO much time and energy and am not seeing the results I want." Every time you step into self-doubt, you give away your power. You literally manifest your struggle even more.

Negative Self-Talk

As a child I learned to be perfectionistic, critical and negative about myself. I was never satisfied with myself. I ended up feeling little self-worth, incapable and fearful about most any situation. I believe I became a perfectionist because of the underlying belief that I would only be loved and accepted if I got everything right and put everyone else's needs first. I put on a brave outer mask to hide behind.

I projected a confidence about myself that just wasn't true. Whenever I did not do as well in school as I expected to or had conflicts with friends, it was automatic for me to think I was at fault. I thought I didn't study the right way, or I had to let other people always be right.

No Sense of Self-Esteem

Even though I had academic success, I never felt I was a success. My family often commented on my appearance, implying I was overweight and ate too much. I felt sad and ugly. Who would love or want to be friends with a fat child?

Years later, I saw pictures of myself with my sister and we weren't overweight at all! I don't know why people made those comments. My sister and I were pretty girls who looked to be of normal weight in most pictures. However, I never felt pretty as a child. When things were good, they weren't good enough, and disaster might be around the next corner. When things were bad, it was a confirmation of what I knew would happen. I dreaded just about everything.

I Burned My Bridges

I'd like to tell you a personal story. I always thought I had my life in rather good order when I was a young adult. When I was around thirty years old, my life fell apart. I had a job I loved and was good at, I had a good salary, I had interesting hobbies, but my personal life was in chaos. I felt emotionally and spiritually isolated. I was going through a divorce and felt like a huge failure because my private life was in such turmoil. I was in such emotional pain that I stopped thinking rationally for a while. I was going through life like a robot, unable to face the fact that my emotional pain and feelings of unworthiness were causing me to spiral out of control.

I made a life-changing decision. Out of the blue I quit my job in Canada and moved to the United States to be with a new love interest. I consulted nobody, asked for no help and I ended up burning all my bridges. I horrified friends and family with my irrational actions and I really didn't comprehend what I was doing to my life. I had no job, no savings but I did have a roof over my head.

I believe God was watching over me, but I felt spiritually disconnected and so alone. It was the first time I had been in such emotional pain and distress. Somehow, I thought that doing a "geographical relocation" was going to be the answer. Guess what, it wasn't. I brought myself and my problems with me. Nothing had changed, only where I lived.

I didn't know that I wasn't thinking or behaving irrationally. I just thought I was going to follow my heart and start enjoying adventures of doing what I wanted and not what others wanted or expected me to do.

I didn't take the time to find out what it took to move to another country and get a job there. I just packed up and moved. I found out I had to be sponsored and have a work visa to get a job, even though I had excellent experience and recommendations.

What an eye-opener. I spent several weeks looking for a job and was blessed to be hired by a wonderful international company that was able to sponsor my work application. That was the beginning of a new start for me. I went on to spend twelve excellent years in the United States for which I have always been thankful. I got a chance to get my life in order, I asked for help and I was able to come through this experience a stronger and wiser person.

I Learned to Ask for Help

I had always considered myself a rational person who led an orderly life. However, when you look at my personal story, it's obvious that I was deeply gripped by chaos and I was afraid to see what was really going on. Thankfully, I was able to get love and guidance from others and my life got back on track.

I found out what was essentially important to me, what excited me, and I had the possibility to set my life on a new path. I am thankful to this day that I made the changes I did, but I still feel the effects of the chaotic way that I went about making that change.

My Life Changed

Several years ago, I was ready for a change in my career. I trained to become a life coach after leaving a long-term job with the United Nations. During these studies I found out about an intriguing energy healing modality called Tapping or EFT (Emotional Freedom Technique).

I had some sessions with an excellent practitioner. I gained clarity and understanding of the root cause of my fears and low self-confidence. What an awakening as years of inner guilt, shame and never feeling good enough diminished. I felt like I was seeing the world through new eyes. My negative thoughts, feelings, anxiety and need to be perfectionistic were hugely diminished. I felt light and free.

I was so excited about Tapping that I decided to add it to my skills as a coach. My niche and my focus were now centred on holistic coaching, working with the body, mind and spirit aspects of clients. I finally realized that I had come into my true self-identity. I knew my purpose and why I was here on earth. I was finally a complete masterpiece. I finally felt capable to build the life I had always wanted, to carry on with the existence I should have lived. The ability to succeed is now a strong core belief I have developed.

Life Is Wonderful Now

The message I hope to share through my story is the same message I bring to others through my coaching and training which has also become my theme in life: **Be the best you can be.**

For so much of my life I felt like I was trapped in a prison I had created myself. But did I create it knowingly or was I prisoner in an environment unknowingly created by others – parents and other family members? It's important to know that you CAN change your mindset. If your path in life is not taking you where you want to go, then face your fears.

You can make things happen. The key to success lies in knowing what you want to occur. Plan, then set some easy goals and get started.

If your mindset isn't right, your life doesn't work. Are you feeling stressed and out-of-balance? Do you have no time for yourself, family and friends? Do you want to find an easy way to let go of stress and have a life of joy and ease? Do you find it hard to say no? Do you want to find your passion, what you really want to do in your life? It's never too late to change.

Addressing Your Fears

Fear about changing can be linked to a past event. If you feel anxious to change, where does that dread originate from? What occurred in your past that set you up for this fear? What has happened in the past to color your experience?

When we are transforming, we may have a "personality struggle". The old set of behaviors were comfortable, and change is scary. It takes time to get accustomed to new ways and actions.

Without a strong sense of self, it's difficult to have solid connections to other people. If you don't know who you really are, you may develop trust issues. You may dread that people who get close to you may eventually reject you.

I wish I could tell you it was easy; I wish I could tell you that all you could desire is within your reach – and it can be. However, there is some work involved. Not the heavy lifting kind, no. For now, let's just say that learning how to have a strong sense of your identity requires courage to get clear on who you are.

Some Wisdom to Share

The most important things that I learned is to always be your authentic self and be open to change. Life has happened for you. And there are many different experiences that you've encountered, but never, ever apologise for who you are and what you've gone through. You never have to be ashamed of anything that you've been through. And I want you to always remember, if you don't remember anything else, lift your head up high and know that everything that you've been through was never wasted. It will not be wasted.

Look at your strengths, interests, talents, what gets you excited to go out to work. Be in a quiet place, write down what excites you in life, who you admire and why. What are you good at? These answers will show you clues to get on the way to a wonderful new life.

I'd like to share some suggestions about how to handle change in your life. As I was writing about what I went through so many years ago, I felt like I relived all the trauma and pain again. I hope the suggestions I set out for you here can help spare you going through the struggles I went through.

1. **Define Your Ideal Self**

Define who you would like to be in the future. List clearly all the traits and behaviors you would like in your life. This image may change several times. Imagine nothing is impossible. This "future you" gives you a focus point to work towards.

2. **Find Your Passion**

Make a list of all the things that you would like to do, study or even resume doing. Think back when you were a child and what you loved to do or what you dreamed of being. Put no restrictions on your imagination and have fun with this.

3. **See What Is Holding You Back**

Try to be honest here. You may not like some of your personality traits, but they can be changed. You need to see what holds you back and then decide what you can do to change things, if possible. Try not to compare yourself with others. This can be demotivating. A better measure would be to shift your focus on where you currently are and compare it to how far you've come.

4. **Define Your Fears**

Three of the most common fears are the fear of the unknown, fear of failure, and fear of *looking* like a failure. It results in your comfort zone trying to keep you safe and secure in what you know and what you are familiar with. Yet, you cannot grow in your comfort zone. Because guess what? You don't know what you don't know (that lies beyond your comfort zone). Push against those barriers, take one action step at a time, which could be as simple as just starting. Use the momentum to carry you through.

5. **Stop Thinking Negatively**

If you notice a negative thought, practice saying "Stop". Replace it with a positive thought. You are usually the one holding yourself back.

Refuse to let those negative thoughts have power over you. It can be an effort to train your mind into this routine, but it is an important part of your journey. Accepting the positive will drive you forward.

6. Have a Support Network

People around us have a huge effect upon our success and what we achieve in our lives. Think about the people you spend your time with. They may be family members, friends or colleagues. Do they have a positive impact on your life? Do they build you up, challenge and support you? You can't always escape work colleagues or family members, but even understanding the impact that they have on you is an important start.

7. Try New Activities

Learning something new is one of the best ways to break out of your comfort zone. It challenges any underlying fears you may have. Attempt to learn something new each day or each week. Variety is the spice of life.

8. Set a Goal or Goals for Yourself

Choose one new area or project and define goals about how you will achieve this. Make sure the goal is specific, measurable, achievable, relevant and has a time deadline. This prepares you for success.

9. Learn to Say No

It may be new to you or a bit difficult but put your needs first. It's vital to look after yourself. Saying no is fine. Your needs are important too. Take some time out to take a course, travel or try a new hobby you've always wanted to learn. This will help you to revitalise yourself.

> *"I cannot say whether things will get better if we change; what I can say is they must change if they are to get better."*
> – Georg C. Lichtenberg

Be the best you can be,

About the Author

Carol Davies is a success strategist coach at Passion Motivator Coaching since 2007. Her passion is to help busy, stressed entrepreneurs find a gentle, easy way to change their life so that they can find out what they really want in their personal and professional lives. Carol and her clients will work as a team to design a personalised plan to set positive goals that takes them to their desired results. She believes that change is not easy, but everyone deserves to have the best life possible.

Carol is well known for her innovative approaches to help her clients clear their resistance to change and get the life they have only dreamed of. She uses a mixture of holistic modalities such as life coaching, neuro-linguistic programming, EFT (Emotional Freedom Technique), Tapping and the Balance Procedure, among others.

Carol has worked in several countries as a manager and researcher with the United Nations. She loves travel and adventure, and her dear tortie cat Zoe.

Her favorite mottos are "Just DO it!" and "Live your best life now!"

> *"I am at my best when I am given the opportunity to help others and do what I love in the process."*
> – *Tanner Clark*

Passion Motivator Coaching

Website: www.thepassionmotivator.com

Email: coachcaroldavies@gmail.com

Facebook: https://www.facebook.com/Caroldaviesthepassionmotivatorl/

Instagram: https://www.instagram.com/thepassionmotivator/

LinkedIn: https://www.linkedin.com/in/caroldaviesthepassionmotivator/

Twitter: https://www.twitter.com/freeyourspirit/

YouTube: https://www.youtube.com/channel/UCJ0PjwSGOXFdgYXFldsgDEA

Pinterest: https://pinterest.com/thepassionmotivator/

Dedication

To my dearest Duncan, thank you for always loving and supporting my aspirations and dreams. You have always been my dearest love and friend.

Chapter Eight

How to Reconnect With Your Life Purpose After Abandonment
by Maylin Lim
Quantum Leap Healer & Relationship Coach, Brisbane, Australia

"Take the steering wheel from the inner child, to be a mature, healthy, happy adult."
– *Maylin Lim*

First Abandonment: Being Sent Away for Adoption

I was born into the Yap family of twelve children as the tenth child. Even though there were two younger brothers who came after me, I was the only child in the family who was sent away for adoption by my oldest aunt. That was my first heartbreak – being unwanted and unloved. The question that always played on my mind was "Why me? There must be something wrong with me!"

I have blurry memories of my first three years of life with my adoptive family, but I do recall those years as warm. I felt welcomed and adored. But the story took a huge twist when I turned three.

At Three, Second Abandonment: My Adoptive Father Leaving Us

Frequent quarrels between my adoptive parents became more intense. The words "money" and "bad woman" were mentioned a lot. I could feel the family was falling apart and my parents were driving each other crazy. The atmosphere was frightening for a little girl who did not understand the adult's world yet. I felt unsafe.

One day, the scene turned into a horror movie when I witnessed a physical fight between my adoptive parents. My mother held up a meat cleaver and, in a raging voice, yelled at my father, "I would rather kill you than let you leave this family!"

I was shocked, crying and panicking, my body trembling as I watched the frightening scene in front of a three-year-old me. Helpless and hopeless, I lost my soul in that moment as I sensed the world that I knew ending – once again.

Fortunately, my brother came home in time to stop the tragedy. But the damage to me emotionally was done, cemented by my adoptive father leaving that day. That marked my second heartbreak – being abandoned by him.

From then on, he only ever came home for a brief visit once a year, on every second day of Chinese New Year. My mother was sad and bitter, feeling like she had lost a big part of herself on that fateful day when he left. Still, my mother used to send me to ask for money from my father. I felt humiliated. No wonder it became so hard for me to ask for help throughout my life.

At the age of sixteen, I was in for another shock. A biological sister I never knew I had called to say that I was adopted! I hadn't known. She told me that my biological father had died and I was expected to attend his funeral. Until then, I'd thought that man was my uncle.

I understood much later that my mother had never told me the truth because she feared I would leave her. My conscience told me to stay loyal to my adoptive mother and not let her know I knew I was adopted. I swallowed my pain of separation from my biological family in silence for many more years.

As a consequence, I subconsciously and intentionally stayed away from both mothers when I left high school. I kept as minimal contact with them as I could, so that I would not upset either for being "disloyal". At the same time, I felt like I belonged nowhere and felt extremely lonely all the time, even when surrounded by people.

There was certainly a lot I picked up and perceived about life, about myself, about people, from these childhood traumas. They laid the foundations for how I would live my life and relate with the people around me over the next four decades.

My survival instinct was keen, always wanting to be outstanding, to prove my self-worth, to be a good girl, to make a lot of money, to keep my mother happy. I became the champion people pleaser, very compromising and tolerant, always worrying about others' opinions of me. Whenever something went wrong in life, I would first blame myself for not being good enough. I would often sugar coat things to look better than they really were.

I was always cautious about letting people know that I was adopted. I feared intimacy and even close friendships. I would cut people off when they were getting "closer" and beginning to know more about me. Yes, I put on different armours, shields and masks to play the "safe" life game. I was very good at it.

Third Abandonment: My Husband Walking Out From Our Marriage

Then in 2015, my husband decided to walk out of our seventeen-year marriage, leaving me and our two beautiful kids. This was my third heartbreak from being abandoned again. It was a huge wake-up call that emotionally took me over the edge!

I felt like all the hidden feelings and emotions from my early childhood traumas were being pulled out of me, all at once, telling me that I couldn't hide "me" – the hurt child – anymore. She was needing immediate attention, or she would die. The message was clear.

I Just Want to Finish the Pain

In 2016, I took action. First, my kids and I relocated from Sydney to Brisbane, knowing only two friends to help us start a brand-new life. But out of desperation to pick myself up again, to survive, I made many unconsciously bad decisions with business and investments that made my life even more painful. I blamed myself even more, so much so that I wanted to give up on me and finish the pain.

I blamed myself for not being able to keep my kids' father for the family. I felt like my heart had been sliced into tiny pieces and thrown out of the window. I was feeling very unappreciated and unworthy.

Looking back now, I was so blessed to have my beautiful son and daughter with me. I was totally out of balance with my body, mind and soul. My relationship with them became very challenging, as if the connections were broken. It was functioning but it felt like something was missing …

Dived Deep to Reconnect with My Life Purpose

I told myself, "Enough is enough! I need to stand up for myself. I need to live my life, to set a good example to my children." I needed to show them that life after divorce can be renewed and relived.

I decided to redeem myself and to redefine who I truly am and live life on my own terms. To do that, I knew I needed to heal myself through being brutally honest with my inner world. I had to find and listen to my inner child whom I had always ignored. I knew the techniques. I'd already taught them for years, and had used them successfully with clients, and even on some issues with myself in the past.

But the Universe had brought me to my knees to reveal much deeper things within me that needed restoring. It was time to walk my Truth even more – for the healing of myself, my family, my clients and ultimately humanity.

When I faced my inner child, she was in so much pain. Hurting from being unseen, unnoticed, unwanted, unloved, unaccepted, alone, helpless, hopeless and lost for so long. As I delved deeper into my inner world, what I discovered underneath the emotional turbulence was a smouldering volcano of old emotions and beliefs – garbage – hidden in my subconscious mind, hindering me from living a happy, successful and healthy life. It was time to extract it all:

1. I had been carrying huge emotional baggage for five decades. No wonder I was always protective, putting on a mask, not able to be sociable. My heart closed me off from getting close to people for fear of being hurt. I realise that it is not that love was never available; I had been pushing people away, including my family and siblings.

2. I had felt guilty about being happy in my marriage when my adoptive mother was not happy in hers and believed that I would lose my husband too. Later when my mother lived with us, I even forbade myself to have closeness with my husband.

3. When my biological parents gave up on me, I made the unconscious decision to not ever be too close to my own children. I always gave my all to my work and business, and taking care of my children was like a chore, just a duty and responsibility as a mother. There was such a lack of bonding, which made my children feel unloved as well, just like my feeling of being unloved by my biological parents and my adoptive mother who was always emotionally absent.

4. I had worked so hard to change my adoptive mother's life, to make her happy. But when she died, unhappy, at age eighty-six, I realised that I had destroyed all that I had earned and had wasted all my money. What was hidden in my mind was, "What's the point? She was not happy anyway. I have failed to be a good daughter to her."

5. My adoptive father was a good man, and yet he left us; hence, I was always very suspicious of men. Therefore, I had built a wall between myself and the men in my relationships to avoid getting hurt. I eventually realised that I had married for the wrong reasons – social expectations, not love. I knew that if I wasn't married by thirty, I would be seen as weird in my society, a misfit.

All of these fears from my childhood trauma also manifested themselves in my physical body as cysts and fibroids in my reproductive system, lumps in my breast (removed twice) and scoliosis (a sign of carrying too much burden that is not mine).

Although I did not believe in stories having a happy ending, at the end of my healing, my story did have one. I transformed my life. I have renewed, reinvented and revived my life like a brand-new person. How did I do it?

To cut a long story short, I have done everything in my power to heal and to practice self-love and self-care. My self-healing approach was multi-pronged:

- Practicing Family Constellation therapy – to free myself from family system dynamic and healed childhood trauma.

- Quantum Healing Hypnosis Therapy – to connect to my higher self and seek higher guidance to live in my true purpose.
- Meditation, regular exercise and healthy diet – to regulate my body, mind and spirit to ensure they are in balance.
- Being mindful of what I feed into my system by filtering what I hear, see and do, and the language I use.
- Renewing my social group by connecting with like-minded, positive people.
- Spending time in nature.
- Doing things that follow my heart as my GPS – things that make me express my truest self with joy, love, peace and a sense of fun.

I am not going to lie; these actions needed, and still need, some intentional effort and hard work. I reassure you that it is worth it when you can come out the other side and shine again. I feel like I have lived two different lives. Everything happens for a purpose; all experiences are like my subjects to learn and assignments to be completed on Earth School for evolution – for my own evolution and humanity's.

I now feel grounded, peaceful, trusting and focused. I have clarity, am mindful and am moving forward from strength to strength. The past is rather painful but at the same time interesting. And I have no regrets as I have always given my best, genuinely and wholeheartedly, in the process. And I learnt some transformative lessons and skills to help others!

I managed to walk out of my comfort zone to promote my work online and offline in helping my clients in their healing and to transform and evolve their lives. Thanks to technology, instead of working with my clients face to face and in group settings, I now can work with clients in various countries: Australia, Singapore, Malaysia, Hong Kong, China and Indonesia.

My clients are from all walks of life, wanting to seek a breakthrough to uncover their potential and new possibilities in life. That is what I am most passionate about and have enjoyed doing for the past 10 years. I have lost count of how many people I have helped, using the same techniques that I used on myself and am qualified to practice.

Some of my clients still keep in touch with me and thank me for my assistance 10 years prior that changed their lives. There has not been a boring moment doing this work that I love, and I shall continue to do this for the rest of my life.

Even my love life has transformed. I have opened my heart again and found a supportive loving partner whom I have been with for two-and-a-half years now. We have learnt so much from each other as East meets West, and together we have four beautiful kids. Our relationship will continue to grow and flourish.

You see, the importance of living our lives purposefully means that not only will we be in alignment with our inner intelligence, inner wisdom and inner knowing, we will also become naturally attractive and influential in whatever we do. When our relationships are successful with ourselves and others, all other successes will follow suit, be it money, parenting, couple relationships, business, career, health, family and so on.

Have you felt or experienced abandonment in some part of your life? Abandoned by family? Teachers? Employers? Even by yourself? My heart goes out to you. I want to reassure you that it is our choice to turn trauma into a gift for us to explore our unlimited possibilities and to be the best version of ourselves, no matter what. Traversing your Earth School – life – in alignment with your purpose is possible, and it is made easier with an attitude of gratitude. I am now so grateful to my two sets of parents and my ex-husband – and even my three abandonment experiences. It has all played a role in learning and evolving in my Earth School.

Like me, you may have some revealing, healing and letting go to do. Letting go is hard; but hanging on is worse. Know that when you experience that reconnection with yourself and purpose, life takes on a whole new colour. I believe that we are all designed to evolve in, and ultimately graduate from, our Earth School with a quantum leap!

> *"We are here to attend Earth School for our Evolution."*
> *– Maylin Lim*

With love and gratitude,

Maylin Lim

About the Author

Maylin is an entrepreneur, author, facilitator and healer who has helped thousands of clients and workshop participants to transform their lives through private sessions and group settings since 2006. She is also a mother to a teenage son and daughter.

Maylin and her ex-husband were the founders of Oneness Academy, a self-development and transformation centre in Malaysia, opened in 2006. They pioneered the introduction of Family Constellation work throughout Malaysia and Singapore, and hosted training by the founder Bert Hellinger (Germany), and many other experienced trainers from Germany, USA, Spain and Taiwan, in order to certify new facilitators

For fifteen years, Maylin travelled around Taiwan, Hong Kong, China, Singapore, Spain and Germany to equip herself with professional skills in coaching and healing. Her favourite modalities are Systemic Constellation, Quantum Healing Hypnosis Techniques, Akashic Records Healing and Mayan (Tzolkin) Calendar Consultation.

Maylin Healing

Website: maylinhealing.com
Email: maylin@maylinhealing.com
Facebook: https://www.facebook.com/MaylinHealing
Instagram: https://www.instagram.com/maylin001/?hl=en
LinkedIn: https://www.linkedin.com/in/maylin-l-092aa8117/

Dedication

This chapter is dedicated to my adoptive mother who didn't get the right support for her divorce process; my siblings who helped me in many ways when I hit rock bottom; our children who love me unconditionally; and all my spiritual warrior friends out there who have been there for me and still are.

Chapter Nine

The Greatest Lesson I Learned as a Coach
by Petros Galanoulis
Author, Speaker, Trauma Counsellor & Life Improvement Coach, Australia

"If you turn up, perform at a level that honours your effort to turn up."
– *Petros Galanoulis*

Revelations

I'd like to share with you the greatest lesson I have learned as a coach, but before that, there is something else you will need to understand.

There is a perception and somewhat truth that those who decide to go into a career of "service to others", such as coaches, psychologists, natural therapies and many more, do it at the expense of themselves, kind of like martyrs to a cause. Why wouldn't they? After all, if they are going to stand for the good of others then there is no time to think of yourself. Isn't that selfish after all? Saying you are there for others but thinking of yourself by having a spa day or doing a fun activity while you do it? How can you be at service for others and also think of yourself? Are you an "other"?

When I first started as a personal crisis coach, I was going through hell, life as I knew it was no longer familiar to me nor was it working for me, I had hit rock bottom on all levels.

Ironically, I was at the lowest point in my life and the beginning of my awakening. In fact, it was that whole journey and my natural curiosity regarding the dynamics of it all that got me into the industry I so love. What I didn't realise yet is how those lessons would tie in with what I would eventually learn through coaching. In fact, I would call these eye openers and life changers, given the effect they would have on my skills and clients.

Blindfolds I Couldn't See

It is so easy to get lost in our mission to serve, out of a passion to help others. This is admirable and a great way to live. However, when is it too much? When is it more about you and unresolved feelings of either guilt or not being good enough? Yes! I did just say that, we often sacrifice ourselves in the name of what we do, we try to do it all, even outsourcing things that are our weakness seems to tall a task.

We immerse ourselves into our service and before we know it, we utter these words, "Oh my goodness! Another year gone, they get faster each year!" Ever spoken those words? Noticed how tired you feel as well at the end of each year that zooms by? We all have at some point and this may seem initially a good thing, because after all, a busy life is a sign of a good life, right? Yes and no.

Consider what makes you a great practitioner, it's your passion, YOU, and also your life experience. Experience gained by time and the opportunity you gave yourself to build your life references. This is something critical to life and something we get in our younger years, but as we move deeper in to our service years, our obligations years, that is the years where our responsibilities like paying bills and fending for a family or partner, and navigating a career takeover, we tend to let go of this experience creation either totally or mostly.

What we do is admirable, noble and divine, but if we are to keep doing it to our best capacity, we need to understand, realise, admit and resolve some things. Having the awareness that when we push ourselves too far, or burn ourselves out, in most cases, that's you chasing perfection or in other words: wanting to be perfect. But that's just it, perfection, if you have not realised, simply does not exist and is essentially a sign of low confidence and self-esteem.

The English naturalist Charles Darwin stated in his book *The Origin of Species* that all species of organisms arise and develop through the natural selection of small, inherited variations that increase the individual's ability to compete, survive and reproduce. You see by the sheer nature of evolution, everything must evolve or perish. And us humans are no different. This makes perfection unattainable and inconceivable, and perhaps not preferable.

Think of a time you stagnated or felt stuck in your life or situation, despite everything being good and done well. The reason you felt stagnant was because that's our natural triggers that urge us to grow. Yet, at the time you would have sworn that things were perfect.

For many of us, perfection is also used as an excuse to punish and criticise ourselves for not doing things "right" and essentially telling ourselves that we are not good enough and therefore undeserving. To top it off we then also put ourselves down and criticise our lack of perfection. Many studies show that it is compensation for a lack of self-esteem.

You may be familiar with the thoughts: "If I don't do the best", "If I don't help my client" and "If I don't give 100% of me and what I have 100% of the time", then "I can't possibly be worthy of this person, their time and money." It's the lashing many of us give ourselves in our pursuit to be great at what we do.

Underbelly

Or is this just our excuse when really, after some point is it to be accepted and acknowledged. There is beauty and purpose in everything in all of us. Consider for the moment a Lamborghini, it looks great, goes awesomely and makes a fantastic sound when it's performing. It performs because it has the right fuel and oil, a tuned and powerful engine, the right pedals in the right place and again all its parts tuned for optimal performance. Add to that, a capable driver and it fulfils its purpose at its highest level.

When that Lamborghini needs it, it is put in for a tune up, a service; it's taken out for a spin to make sure it's functioning at optimum level. Now remember we aren't doing all that for the car to be perfect (because there will always be something out there someone will like better or a new model comes out with something different, then at that point the bar is raised again), but so it runs at optimal level and fulfilling its purpose – the basis of an amazing driving experience.

So, what does a car have to do with you? Well, everything in this sense; and here is how. You have a beauty about you, it is part of what makes you, YOU! It's also part of what makes you the great practitioner/service provider, you also have a purpose to fulfil and as you know, it's no coincidence that you are doing what you are doing or pursuing the path you are choosing as your life's work.

Now imagine you are the driver of that beautiful Lamborghini flooring it down a wondrous coastal road, ocean on one side, bushland on the other. You do this every day for weeks on end and as time goes on, various parts of the car start to wear and tear, lose their tune. You notice this because the Lamborghini isn't quite driving the same, it's now harder to reach levels of performance it used to reach with less effort. It's burning more oil and petrol and just not performing as it used to.

But you can't stop, you have a job to do and that is to drive this Lamborghini, it's what you do, although now you are starting to wish you didn't. Your fuel is running low and the engine is performing poorly and you are starting to resent your purpose because you aren't fulfilling it at your best. It's become overwhelming and not fun …

War of the Inner Worlds

Why am I doing this again you wonder? At this point, ask yourself what are you giving? How are you living as you are giving? If you are to keep giving and living in tune with your beauty and purpose, then you must practice Positive Selfishness!

The law of "Positive Selfishness" stated that how we look after ourselves spiritually, mentally and physically is the sole determinant of the quality of our life, our communication AND our output! If we are "off" on the inside, then everything on the outside will also be "off".

I have a little saying I learned, "although noble, giving all of *You* at the expense of yourself is actually more detrimental to the success, well-being and prosperity of you, your loved ones and your work." One must learn to practice Positive Selfishness to ensure that you remain valuable to yourself, your work and your loved ones. But this does not mean that you should be obnoxious, self-centred or arrogant.

What it means is that the minute you start tending, pleasing and giving to yourself and not neglecting yourself, you start to truly become a valuable person to those you care about. It is invaluable that you are healthy in all senses, fulfilled and happy, satisfied and that you are giving enough to yourself that you have the strength, endurance and energy and therefore want and presence; to be there for those you care about when they need you.

To positively give to yourself is to proclaim that you deserve it and are worth it, and when you believe it, so will others. The scales are only level when both sides are balanced. Once one side gets too much, the scales tip, so will you if you deny yourself in the name of whatever … No, no, no. To keep firing on all cylinders you must be constantly making time to tune up, physically, mentally and spiritually. Complete harmony means excellent output. In other words, it's from the heart, it's conscious giving, its energetically affordable and able to be given without it putting a strain on you.

Awakening

At the start of this piece I told you about a great lesson I learned through serving in the coaching, counselling and personal development industry. Well here it is and why understanding the above is important. I have been asked by up and coming coaches and those thinking about getting in to coaching and counselling, "What makes a great coach?"

At first, I was never really sure how to answer that exactly. Was it their years of experience or their knowledge? Was it their ability to listen or ask great and appropriate questions? All of these are valid questions, especially the last one, which I hail as my second greatest lesson I learned through coaching.

However, the greatest lesson I learned through coaching is that when I'm sitting in a room with a client ready to coach them, there are actually two clients in the room, not just one. Yes, you as the coach are also the client. When you are coaching the person in front of you, you are also coaching the person within you and so what you advise and discuss with your clients, you effectively and by default virtually must prescribe to yourself.

Give yourself the time to be someone other than the coach, be the client, be the person who needs a breakaway task to refuel and actually does it. Be the person who takes a trip every so often or the person, who once a month goes to the opera. Do something completely different and something that you truly love.

Just understand that to be your best at Positive Selfishness, you must give yourself a chance to practice on yourself. Schedule time for reflection, see your own coach or counsellor, have a breakaway hobby where you can be you and keep that connection to you and wash off your clients' negative energy.

Have breaks to explore other things at scheduled intervals so as to rejuvenate and to miss it a little.

Sometimes we get so immersed in something that we burn ourselves out and may come to resent what we do even if we love it. Some variety and small breaks keep the flame lit and the heart ever so fond. This means that our output is at its best.

> *"Martyrs die; at that point, they are no good to themselves, their loved ones or their cause."*

You see, we are not given a purpose in life to simply fulfil just ourselves, we are given a purpose to find ourselves and so as to also be a special moment in time in others' lives, which fate brings together to unlock something in them for their own journey. We are one of the cogs in the universe that goes to work for others calling upon the power of the universe in just the same way as we do for our life.

Greyer With Wisdom

If you are attending to yourself like any part or machine, needing a service, then not only are you fulfilling your grand purpose but also helping others do the same. This is why it is important that you live while you give.

I am definitely attending to myself more and, as a result, my business is evolving for the better as well. Coming soon, there will be practical, life-changing 30-day programmes online for free with optional access to a growing library of practical skills, insights and much more. A service that will spread in to the NDIS system to help out those not as fortunate (yet) to afford the support they need; as well as a unique and original retreat that helps people to think, decide and act like a champion when life happens. Also, there may be a book or two more.

There is more to come but not at the expense of me, but in service of me so I can be in service of you.

Paying It Forward

Here are some tips for Positive Selfishness and how you can do this effectively:

- Schedule time slots into a diary or calendar, specifically for You.
- Predetermine how long and frequent this will be and pre-organise for that time to be covered for you, leave no excuses, which includes guilt (bar emergencies) for not taking the time.
- Be selfish in this time (positively, not obnoxiously). The difference is that when being positively selfish you include yourself in the giving with others, and compassion and connection is developed. In the obnoxious way, you exclude everyone else and say to hell with them at any expense.
- Have a pre-made list of things you have compiled over time that you would like to do and get going.
- Have a journal handy and keep a tab of all thoughts and feelings, learnings and experiences.

"The only true hurdle in our life is our self, move out of your way!"
– *Petros Galanoulis*

Live Like You Mean It,

Petros "The Human GPS" Galanoulis

About the Author

Petros Galanoulis is a personal crisis coach and counsellor, helping people solve and recover mentally and emotionally from a personal trauma or crisis. He owns and runs You Got This mental health services.

He is also the author of the nationally acclaimed You Got This: 7 Steps to Effectively Solving Any Personal Crisis Better, Faster and recently released his second book Reaching for The Light: A Path for Deep Healing, Forgiveness and Re-Empowerment After Sexual Trauma.

Based in Melbourne, Australia, he is referred to as the human GPS because of his style of coaching and guidance. He works as a crisis and trauma recovery coach and counsellor, predominantly with individuals who are struggling through a major and difficult life transition or traumatic event.

With over 15 years of professional experience and 35 years of personal experience, he developed his coaching process: the GPS system.

Petros holds a degree in psychology and is working his way to become a full board-certified psychologist. He also holds a diploma in life coaching and counselling, having also studied the spiritual philosophy of Vedanta and is a qualified practitioner of Reiki, hypnotherapy and neuro-linguistic programming.

Petros has appeared in the media, and his personal and professional mission is to help as many people he can to live like they mean it!

Petros is also a practical and inspirational speaker and (sometimes cheeky) thought provoker, always exploring the flipside of life with topics such as:

1. Breaking through "Panic Brain".
2. The three major actions to take when hit by a crisis.

3. The three common things you do normally that you shouldn't do when you have experienced a crisis or trauma.
4. The seven effective steps to navigate through any crisis successfully.

You Got This Mental Health and Personal Improvement Counselling Services

Website: www.yougotthismentalhealth.com.au
Email: coachpetros@gmail.com
LinkedIn: https://www.linkedin.com/in/petrosgalanoulis/

Dedication

To my family, friends, past lovers, mentors, those that have inspired me and those that have bugged me, for making me who I am today.

Chapter Ten

Life Woke Me Up
by Sally Holden

Author, Speaker, Adventurist, Intuitive Life Coach and Creator of the Thrive Program, Australia

"Loving yourself is the best gift you can ever give the world."
– Sal Holden

I was so blessed in my childhood, I grew up with the most wonderful, loving and supportive parents, they were financially successful in their own business. We were truly taught some amazing values and the gift of self-responsibility and working hard to create and have what we wanted in life.

I've always been the typical straight A student type. I was blessed with being able to sail through my academic years excelling in my class. I seemed to have it all and I did …

Except for my self-esteem. I was so used to receiving external validation from others, getting cheered on and receiving extra love or approval for being "successful" or doing well. Soon, it became a relentless drive and pressure as I was unconsciously longing for more and more acceptance, validation and love from those around me.

I had tied it deeply to my external success, my body shape and what others seemed to expect and want from me. I turned myself inside out to be the good girl, to be the people-pleaser and tried to make everyone happy, constantly squashing how I really felt back down inside of myself, often with food and sugar, and putting on the bright bubbly smile on the outside.

Believing that my lovability came solely from the way I looked and how well I performed, I spiralled deeper and deeper into self-loathing.

I met my boyfriend at sixteen. He was the first guy that seemed to "notice" me, and my only thought at the time was that he seems to love me, so he must be the right person for me.

We had a turbulent and very unhealthy on-again off-again relationship. I moved away at twenty years old, later coming back to the relationship, being promised that things had changed. We moved in together and shortly afterwards became engaged and later married.

Fourteen years later, I hit rock bottom, as my life fell completely apart. Years and years of not loving or respecting myself had taken a huge toll. I had burnt myself out completely by trying so desperately hard to be all that I thought he had wanted me to be and living in such a state of fear, trying to be the perfect wife on every level. I'd lost all control of my life and was doing anything I could to maintain the illusion of control, by keeping our house perfect, working four days a week and raising our girls.

I'd totally lost myself. I had no clue who I was, I had lost the spark in my eyes and the fire in my soul. I felt so lifeless and sad, and berated myself for not feeling more grateful as I appeared to have "a great life". I couldn't understand why I was so miserable.

After a weekend away, I came home to a distant husband, who in truth I'd felt distant from for years. I finally summoned up the courage to ask him the question, did he still love me?

He looked me straight in the eye and said, "No." And that was it, with one word spoken, our marriage was over.

Devastated and yet strangely relieved all at the same time, I instantly became a single mum to my two girls aged five and seven years old at the time.

A few short months after that, my beautiful mum was diagnosed with terminal cancer and passed away not long after that.

To say that life had slapped me to the ground and shook me to my core to wake me up is an understatement.

At the time I was only earning $300 a week at a part-time job that I didn't love. I was unhealthy, overweight and lived in total fear, grief, anger and terror that I wouldn't have enough money to provide for my girls, especially to pay for private school tuition.

I was completely burnt out mentally, emotionally and physically.

I felt so alone, I felt that nobody cared, I felt that nobody was there for me. I was drowning in self-pity and shame.

It was a Sunday afternoon, and for the umpteenth time, I was lying in bed, angry at myself, grieving and feeling unable to get up and be with my girls, who were playing in the living room. I hated myself. I hated how I was living. I hated how I felt, I hated who I was being. I hated the kind of role model I was to my girls. Worst of all, I hated that I was allowing all of this.

I made a vow to myself then and there and I drew a line in the sand, with more conviction and determination than I had felt in myself in years. I made a real decision and I said to myself that my girls deserve better than this.

They became my single and sole focus for improving my life. I didn't yet love myself enough to do it for me. But I knew in my heart how deeply I loved them and would do anything for them, and it was the inner resolve I needed to totally transform my life.

I knew that I had to heal my mind, body and soul.

Negative thoughts consumed my mind day in day out. I made a resolve to plug into positive audio every single morning. I knew that if I put positive in, eventually positive would have to start coming out. It was in one of these audios that I heard the statement that changed my life forever.

"My life was the way it was, because of me."

Ouch! I was enraged, didn't they know that my husband had left me, didn't they know my mum had died of cancer, didn't they know how hard it was for me. I was so angry because I thought what they were saying meant that it was *all my fault*.

It wasn't *all* my fault, but it was *my* responsibility, and in truth, I'd created a huge majority of it. My happiness, my wellbeing, my wealth, my life and how I chose to live and feel every day was absolutely MY responsibility.

As the message seeped in over the next few weeks, I could see that my life was the way it was because of the choices I'd made, in how I was choosing (unconsciously at the time) to react, rather than respond to the life events that I was experiencing.

I also learnt that metaphysically adrenal fatigue and burnout are created through patterns of feeling powerless to change a situation or our life. I could see how my entire life and my beliefs, thoughts and feelings had led to my burn-out and how flat and exhausted I felt in myself.

Everything changed when I realised that my responsibility was based upon my *response-ability*.

I knew in my heart, I had to become a master of my emotions and take my reactivity, powerlessness, shame and blame and turn it into choosing to respond, with love, wisdom, integrity and congruence.

I had become so filled with anger and resentment over the years from feeling that I needed to give everything to everyone else and make them all happy, in the hope that I would receive love and appreciation back. In short, I was trading. I was totally dependent on others and what they thought about me, or how they responded to me, for my sense of self-worth and lovability.

I could see that the universe had in fact given me the greatest gift of my life. I know that if I could have my mum back in a heartbeat, I absolutely would want that. However, I also knew at the deeper level of my soul that this had also happened for a reason. I had been totally dependent on my mum's unconditional love to fill my bucket and had also used my intimate relationship as a way of trying to get love.

With neither of these now physically present in my life. I was left with myself to deal with, stripped bare from what seemed to be all other forms of external love, albeit for my girls. But even that sense of love would go missing when they would spend time with their dad.

I knew deep in my heart and my soul, that learning to love myself was the key to getting my life back. I had read enough about the Law of Attraction to know that if I felt unlovable, unworthy or undeserving, there was no way that I was going to be able to change my life. I understood on such a deep level that my previous marriage was the perfect reflection of how I felt about myself.

Over time, I also could see how I had totally created the situation for my husband to leave, as I knew in my heart that we were not aligned. Our values were so vastly different and we wanted completely different things. For the first time, I felt truly grateful as it had actually been a blessing in disguise, and I was also grateful for the good times.

I took my self-responsibility to the next level. I started exploring what I was truly passionate about and enrolled in my Certificate IV in Kinesiology course. I had no clue how I would pay for it, but I said yes and kept affirming that I would make it happen. A couple of weeks later, an ex-employer rang me and asked me if I would like to work for her one day a week. It was for the exact amount that I needed to pay for the course.

I poured positive audio into my mind and heart daily. I read whatever I could about changing my life. I started running, at first it was two kilometres, then five kilometres, then ten kilometres and eventually that turned into fifteen kilometres, then twenty-two kilometres, then seven triathlons. I changed my diet and eating habits to support my recovery.

I started investing in myself, this was a huge stretch, especially when I had to save for three weeks just to take my girls out for ice cream. Investing in myself shifted how much I valued and believed in myself. I often freaked out and was mostly filled with tears and self-doubt, but yet I kept committing and saying yes to what my intuition and my heart was guiding me to do.

I've had so many people I looked up to over the years, the most impactful was Tony Robbins and one of my amazing mentors, Scott Harris. I listened to Tony Robbins every day, so much so that I could even repeat his words verbatim. Having incredible mentors, coaches and teachers that believed in me, even before I could believe in myself, was a true gift.

My kinesiology training was life changing to say the least. My commitment was unwavering which bolstered my self-belief and passion. I completed over thirty-six eleven-hour return trips to complete my kinesiology courses, leaving at two in the morning on a Saturday and coming home at eleven at night on a Sunday. I knew it was time to help other people change their life, too.

Together with my kinesiology and coaching training and a tonne of self-love, I became unstoppable and looked forward to giving to others.

I had healed my body, mind and soul, and I had created my new vision for my life, I knew what I wanted. Being a role model to my girls was my biggest driver by far, but now, I also knew I was doing it for myself.

I had never felt so aligned, driven, clear, passionate and excited about my life. My inner fire had been reignited and I still remember the year I hit my first six-figure income in my business. It was a dream come true. I embraced even more self-love and respect, attracting an incredible relationship, wonderful friends and my continuing business success. My girls are now seventeen and nineteen years old, and to be honest I couldn't be prouder of them.

I'm truly so excited and passionate to be sharing my message of self-love and empowerment with so many other women all over the world, helping them heal from their burnout and adrenal fatigue.

Fatigue, stress and exhaustion truly impacts so many women even in the day-to-day stresses of everyday life, let alone if we are over-giving or over-compensating, putting everyone else's needs first or feeling overly responsible for everyone and everything.

I often see women putting themselves on the backburner, thinking that they will just deal with it all when the kids grow up, often crippling themselves mentally, physically and emotionally for years from the fall out of physical exhaustion and burn out.

That is why I'm so passionate about my Thrive programme that addresses all of these issues and more, to return women to a full state of health, happiness, self-love and truly thriving in life again. For more information on my products and services, as well as free resources (including my free e-book *A Pocketbook of Love – 11 Ways to Love Yourself*), please visit www.abundantheartcoaching.com.

I feel so blessed to be truly living my dream life, location free, thriving in my own way that lights my heart up, and empowers me to radiate love and light into the world.

If you are at a crossroads in your life, and you know deep in your heart that things need to change, I hope that some of my biggest learnings are a gift and a guiding light for you.

1. Self-love is your greatest gift to yourself, to others and to the world. When we truly love ourself, we stop doing things out of resentment and obligation, and start giving from a full bucket in a way that truly lights us up.

2. Self-responsibility will set you free. I truly believe that life is a gigantic mirror, where everything we attract towards us is a reflection of our thoughts, beliefs and how we are feeling every single day. To change our life, we need to first change our thoughts and beliefs.

3. Emotional mastery is king. So many people wait for things to change, so they can feel better, often leaving them feeling powerless. When you know how to change your emotions in a heartbeat and change your emotional response to anything, you now know exactly how to work with the law of attraction.

4. Your physical body is your most precious gift. Make sure you treat it with the kindness, love and respect it deserves. Patterns of dis-ease are messages from your soul, letting you know that something has to change. They will only get louder until you listen to them.

5. Clarity is absolutely key. If you don't know where you are going, it's like trying to drive with a muddy windscreen. You won't know where to turn and you'll be scared of moving forward. Create a vision that lights your heart up and makes you want to sing.

6. Be you, everyone else is taken. You are a unique, precious and vital gift to the world.

"You are the answer you've been looking for."
– Sal Holden

Love and Blessings,

Always in All Ways,

About the Author

Sally Holden is a Speaker, Author, Intuitive Life & Business Coach and previously a Kinesiologist, who is passionate about empowering women to really follow their heart. She has personally assisted thousands of people over the last ten years to improve their health, confidence and wealth, and has been involved in the personal development field for over twenty-three years.

Her greatest gift is being able to intuitively sense what her clients are feeling, combining both transformational mindset processes, strategic action steps and guiding them to have an even deeper inner connection with their heart and soul, in order for them to truly get the results that they desire and deserve.

She is excited to bring her expertise, online programmes, energy and love to more and more women and empower them with effective strategies to master their emotions and live a life they truly love, as well as to recover from adrenal burnout and fatigue.

She has spoken at various community events and facilitated commercial and personal development workshops and women's retreats.

She currently resides in Wagga with her two teenage daughters, living a laptop lifestyle of freedom, sharing travel and hiking fun and adventures with her soul mate, whilst fulfilling her dreams and living her soul's purpose.

Abundant Heart Coaching

Website: www.abundantheartcoaching.com

Email: admin@sallyholden.com.au

Facebook: www.facebook.com/sally.holden3.

LinkedIn: https://au.linkedin.com/in/sally-holden-2a28a746

YouTube: https://www.youtube.com/c/SallyHolden11

Dedication

To my daughters Elissa and Talia, my truest inspiration in life. May you know love, be love and give love and always have the courage to follow your heart. I love you.

Chapter Eleven

My Life as a Jelly Bean
by Sophia Rigas
Author, Psychic & Reiki Master; Australia

"Laughter is more cleansing than tears; though I have great respect for tears."
– Sophia Rigas

I am going to ask you to use your imagination for a minute …

Imagine that you are a young person who has been raised within the nucleus of a loving and caring family. A family that has gone through many ups and downs and know what it means to support, trust and sympathise with each other and the rest of the world. I want you also to imagine that you are intelligent and independent, having been raised to have high ideals and a great sense of humour.

Hello, my name is Sophia and I would like to tell you how I became a Jelly Bean.

At this early point of my life – around my mid-twenties – I was ready to take over the world. I was gutsy, optimistic and full of ideas that I couldn't wait to share with the world. Already I had a diploma under my belt and was beginning to feel constricted by the old traditions and limiting beliefs of my own European country. Wider horizons were beckoning. I then had the chance to come to Australia when my pen-pal and long-time friend who had recently migrated proposed to me. Since I was keen to leave my country, I made the decision to come for better or worse.

In the beginning the family I was introduced into was welcoming and curious to know me better. Soon after the novelty of my arrival faded, I realised that my new life was not as ideal as I'd hoped it would be. I was anxious to fit in and belong in my new family. Yet it turned out that they were distrustful, negative, believed everyone was a liar and thought all others shared similar beliefs. During this time, I felt the only way to survive was to compromise myself and give in to others; sometimes I even felt forced to. I guess it was a coping mechanism.

To give you a clear idea, here are some examples of how I compromised myself:

- I agreed to everything to please others as a reflex action rather than trust my own intuition and intelligence. As Joanna Trollope says, "I've got so used to reacting, I've rather lost the art of acting."
- I set myself up as an easy target to keep the peace.
- I laughed at jokes that were humiliating to myself and others.
- I allowed them to make decisions for my life.
- I gave up practicing art to stop the criticism and ridicule.
- I put myself deliberately below others so I wasn't perceived as a threat.
- I constantly sought approval and was not comfortable accepting compliments or praise.

The bottom line was that I felt I had to keep my mouth shut and be a doormat for the sake of my four children. By this time, I was depressed, emotionally exhausted and even suicidal at times. After 25 years, I reached my limit. It may seem like a long time to some, but to each their own.

Such was my transition into life as a Jelly Bean. Glossy and colourful on the outside, full of smiles and sunshine, whilst on the inside a gooey mess, compressed and moulded to fit in anywhere. What was even scarier was that after I removed myself from that family and filed for divorce, I kept these strategies for years out of habit.

According to the founders of Neuro Linguistic Programming, Richard Bandler and John Grinder, habits and personality issues are formed in our early childhood years or through long repetition, and with our *subconscious awareness and agreement* of what we are doing. I cannot tell when this awareness started but I gradually realised that subconsciously I had made the decision to give up some traits of my personality to adopt meekness and obedience in order to keep the peace and create a more stable family situation.

Ultimately, it was this "selling out" of myself that fuelled my anger and caused me to blame myself, even though it was – on some level – entirely my own choice to be this way. But more on that later.

At the time of my divorce I felt that I had gotten out clean. I thought that because I was no longer within that environment that I was free of it. How wrong I was. Removing myself from the toxic situation never meant for a second that I had removed the toxins from my life.

I was still angry, still felt like a victim and still criticised my ex-husband and in-laws' actions. At no point had I reflected on the role I played. Truth be told, I was utterly oblivious to the fact that I was chock-a-block full of residual emotional baggage. Ask me at the time and I would have sworn black and blue that I was fine and dandy.

It wasn't until years later that I first became aware that something was wrong. I was having a conversation with a good friend when I heard my own ugly accusations reflected back at me. My words coming out of her mouth made me realise how harsh I was being. The strongest feelings I can recall from that moment are shock and shame. I was shocked at the extent of my venom and ashamed at the knowledge that I had become a poorer version of myself.

My in-laws were simply being themselves. They were wrapped up in their own personal problems and I was an easy target. This is what made me angry; an anger that lasted over two decades. The deepest revelation came soon after – when I realised that all this time, I was really angry at myself for allowing it to happen.

I had another revelation: these people weren't the bad guys I painted them to be. Yes, they had their issues, but so did I! Taking ownership of the role I played meant that I had to give up my blame.

Here is my pearl of wisdom … OWN YOUR SHIT!

This marked the beginning of my true freedom. It literally took *one single moment of decision* to take the first step to my recovery. After that the emotional revelations unfolded thick and fast, but none as intense as this first experience.

Once free, I had absolutely no idea who I was; I had forgotten the real me! After the awakening that came with it, I had to reinvent my character and behaviour. It was time to let go of the strategies and behaviours of my old Jelly Bean self. I decided to become …

A Smartie!

Smarties have a firm yet delicious centre full of chocolatey goodness like a tender and compassionate heart. They also have a colourful hard shell that repels all of life's tedious and unnecessary dramas. This new and improved version of myself needed its core values aired, so putting to good use the words of Rahm Emanuel, "never let a good crisis go to waste," here are a few of the gems I learned and applied into my new Smartie self:

- Self-respect: I give to others when my own full cup runneth over, and not before my own thirst is quenched.
- Adaptability and tact: There is power in being able to adapt and be flexible. It can be done in a way that remains true to my values and integrity. Being tactful allows me to do all of the above while considering other people's feelings and maintaining good relationships.
- Resilience: It's as simple as "what doesn't kill you makes you stronger."
- A proper sense of fairness: I do not hold the scales of justice; it is not right to judge others – they have their own journey. Therefore, "let he who hath no sin cast the first stone."
- Humour: Seeing humour in a situation lightens my heart and through the years broke the tension when it became too much to bear. Laughter is more cleansing than tears I think; though I have great respect for tears.

> *"And there is plenty more useful life to be lived and extraordinary things to do ..."*
> – *Sophia Rigas*

All the best,

Sophia Rigas

About the Author

Sophia Rigas is a kindergarten teacher. She came to Australia in 1976 and worked in the family hospitality business for thirty years, establishing five franchises while raising four children.

Sophia has also taught the elderly for twenty-five years, became a public speaker, studied Interior Decoration, Visual Arts, Commercial Art and other minor subjects.

Sophia also discovered Reiki, which allowed her to reconnect with her late mother, a professional Medium. She received information about her own karma, the lessons that she has learnt in this life and why. As a result, her perspective on life changed and she studied and practiced hard to become a Reiki master and teacher. Finally, Sophia studied life coaching and neuro linguistic programming, which took her further than expected and gave her a boost of confidence.

Sophia sought to explore new grounds and allowed herself to come out of the "psychic closet". She engaged her talent as an artist to draw portraits of people's spirit guides. She discovered the Runes and fell head over heels in love with them. For the last six years, Sophia has worked as a psychic and feels privileged to have helped people to help themselves.

Sophia is currently working on her fifth book (including this collaboration), teaching others to decipher the mysteries of the Runes.

Her Jelly Bean self is long gone – that ship has sailed – and her Smartie years are coming to a close. Sophia now looks to establish herself as an M&M with a peanut centre. It's just like being a Smartie really, but with balls!

The Age of Wisdom

Email: srigas502002@yahoo.com.au

Dedication

I dedicate this chapter to my four children.

Every obstacle was worth surpassing for having the great pleasure of seeing you flourish with integrity as capable, compassionate and mature people.

Chapter Twelve

Perseverance, Resilience and the Growth Mindset – A Key Trio
by Cheryl Strickland
Wellness Lifestyle Strategist, Canada

"Let go of who you think you're supposed to be and embrace who you are."
– Brené Brown

Have you ever had a moment in time that you will always remember? Well, I have! It was the end of another work week but I had a special pleasure that I was going to savour. Two weeks of freedom – a long anticipated holiday away from that daily stress and strain of work. It was a Friday in the middle of June. I was smiling and so were my colleagues. All of a sudden, things changed!

We were hastily summoned into a short staff meeting to receive brutal news – our office with more than thirty people was being closed within two months! We were a mix of clerical and technical workers in a large telecommunications company.

Only a small percentage of the technical people were being offered the chance to transfer to a new venue two hours away. No jobs were offered to the clerical support staff! I was in the clerical staff with many years seniority and now looking at possible unemployment.

My Life Was Out of Control

This situation was a crisis for me personally and professionally. I was catapulted into a new life adventure! I had many years of tenure with my company. A million questions raced through my mind! Why me? What was I going to do? I experienced feelings of loss, betrayal and of being in free-fall. I ran the gamut of emotions: panic, self-doubt, uncertainty, depression and rage. I did not deserve what was happening to me.

Well, for me, giving up and total panic was not the answer. I decided to focus on the future and its possibilities; I had to put ME first. I had to find a positive solution. I definitely knew that I was not to blame for what was happening so I decided to get my act in gear to see what I could do. I embraced all of those negative feelings, acknowledged them and then let them go. I found out what kind of person I was when I started looking at how I was going to successfully survive this calamity.

How I Faced My Fears

I never expected to lose my job after being there for so many years. It wasn't part of my safe and secure world. I literally didn't know what to do or where to turn. I felt sheer terror for a few moments and then I realised that staying stuck in fear was not an option. So, I made a list of those fears:

- Must move to another city.
- Traumatic life transition involving personal loss with resulting emotional impact.
- Give up current friends, residence and comfort zone.
- Have to establish myself in a new environment.
- Can I do all this?

Once I clarified my fears, I felt a tremendous sense of calm and purpose. I knew what I had to do to move forward to get a new and better job.

I Found a Solution

My personal breakthrough occurred midway during my struggles to find a new, positive life. I found the needed self-confidence to approach people and ask for help. I knew I had solid qualifications to offer so I made that known. I was lucky to find out that a special board of top-level executives was coming to my city to interview candidates for the technicians' lateral transfer.

A light bulb went off in my head when I heard this news. I had more than enough job knowledge and experience to act as a valuable adjunct to this department. I personally knew the top executive who managed my current department, so I made an appointment with him and pitched myself and my experience. I said that I am an asset to this company and would like to have a chance to transfer to the new city. He liked my positive attitude and arranged a special interview for me. I was proud of myself for speaking up and being self-confident.

I Found My Self-Confident Mindset

I found out that I was resilient – I went to senior management and pitched myself. I convinced them why I was an asset and valuable to the company. I developed a professional support network that included mentors and job contacts. I saw a move to a new city as an exciting opportunity both personally and professionally. I welcomed change. My old job was actually rather boring and one that I had tolerated for years. These new positive feelings of challenge and excitement energised me. I was going to win and find a better career experience.

My upbeat and confident attitude was immediately noticed when I had my interview. I brought a different type of energy in with me and everyone remarked that I had a great smile! What was my immediate result? I was offered the choice of three excellent positions and I was driven around in a company car to see what appealed to me. I was very excited and my personal self-assurance grew in leaps and bounds. I chose a very stimulating position that was a great fit for my experience and talents. Another perk was meeting a wonderful set of new co-workers. I did it! I found an amazing new future.

Accepting What Happens

Whether you've already lost your job through downsizing, redundancy or any other reason, or if you're under threat to lose your job, your first thoughts run from blind panic to anger, desperation, and all points in between, especially if you have a family and all the commitments that go with it.

It is especially daunting if you've been in that position for a long time and assumed that you had that job for life. When it's the only job you've ever known, finding out that it's gone can be devastating.

Even if it's a job that you've tolerated for years, when you no longer have it, you suddenly forget all the things that you didn't like about working there and remember only the good. It's human nature.

But the feelings of loss and being in free-fall create feelings of doubt, and doubt can cause a huge loss in self-confidence at a time when you need it the most.

Rather than block out those feelings, acknowledge them, embrace them and then let them go. They will not serve you in moving forward.

Keep in mind that many layoffs are activated by accountants – usually people you don't know and have never met. They have no idea who you are, what your skills are, what your true worth is, and how your family might suffer from your job loss. They're just doing the job that they're paid to do.

Why Me?

Granted, it might be tough for you to make sense of the situation. But sooner or later, you know that you have to get past it, over it or around it, so why not make it sooner? Later has no merit at all, does it?

Here's the truth. Losing a job is part of modern society. We live in a rapidly changing world, and this is just another kind of change, and change is the only constant we can truly expect.

Look around you. Everyone you know that has a job has come from some other workplace. And most of them ended up with a better job after their move! You can too!

Regardless of what happens to you, it's what you do about what has happened to you that's important.

So, although you didn't anticipate this change, you can look at it as an opportunity to rethink, reset, adjust and get a clear idea of not only what is possible for you, but what could also change your life for the better.

Have you ever had thoughts about a career change? It just might be the perfect time to consider one. It could be so much easier to make such decisions now that your old job isn't holding you back from going after what you truly desire.

Could There Be a More Perfect Time?

Think about it. Could there be a more perfect time to redefine what you want to do with your life and be clear on what's important to you?

Follow these steps to plan your perfect direction:

1. Decide what you want to avoid. An easy place to start is with what you DON'T want, and then look at the opposite.

    » For example, if you totally loathe commuting, look at a role where you could work from home. Tens of thousands of people already do, why not you too?

2. What about your chosen field of expertise? If you're tired of that kind of work, maybe you could look at something completely different.

    » You can find free courses on the internet for thousands of different skill sets. Sign up for as many as you need to get an understanding of what's out there that just might be a perfect fit for you.

3. Explore new ideas using your current interests. Consider anything and everything that gets your attention. Start paying close attention to what interests and fascinates you. There could be something within arm's reach that you've had an interest in for some time. For example:

> - If you go to the bookstore, which sections do you visit most often?
> - If you're channel surfing on the television, what kind of programmes do you stop to watch most often?
> - If you're scrolling social media, what type of stories do you read the most and/or comment on the most?

Make copious notes for a week or more. Then go back and review. Notice where the commonalities are and decide to follow up on what gets your attention the most.

You may find a fascinating new direction to pursue!

Some people have found that losing their job was the best thing that could have happened to them. Why not for you?

What I Learned

When it comes to adversity and facing the problems that we all encounter in our lives, it's important to develop both perseverance and resilience. Both qualities are essential to the growth mindset that we all need to be able to adapt to change and be able to overcome challenges.

There are five steps to developing the growth mindset that you need to develop relentless drive:

- Focusing on your choice of language – giving yourself praise and using language that gives you credit for the effort and strategy that you've put in.
- Surrounding yourself with positive-thinking people to help you develop a positive mindset.
- Adopting flexible patterns of thinking.
- Setting goals that align with your own purposes.
- Building time into every day for reflection.

Just What Are Perseverance and Resilience?

Perseverance is:

- Tenacity.
- Passion for a meaningful long-term goal.
- Commitment to difficult or challenging tasks.

Resilience is:

- The ability to recover from difficult events and bounce back.
- Working through suffering and emotional pain and coming out stronger and more positive.
- Able to tap into personal support systems and strengths to overcome challenges.

Without perseverance and resilience, talent can amount to nothing but unmet potential. It's only when you put in effort that your talents become skills that can lead to success.

The Importance of Resilience and Perseverance to a Growth Mindset

Resilience and perseverance are vital to the growth mindset that is so essential to developing relentless drive in every walk of life to ensure your personal success.

Resilience and perseverance are especially important in the workplace where challenges are especially common. Becoming resilient at work is a skill you can learn.

Resilient employees:

- Build strong connections and relationships with others.
- Are team players.
- Have good communication skills.
- Foster positive emotions with others.
- Engage in self-care to avoid burnout.

- Are true to themselves and behave in ways that align with their own values and beliefs.
- Are determined to achieve ambitious goals.
- Perceive their work as meaningful.
- Are flexible and adaptive to change.

You can develop more resilience by:

- Taking a positive stance.
- Putting energy and motivation into your work.
- Having emotional insight.
- Developing a healthy work-life balance.
- Fostering spirituality.
- Becoming reflective.

Cultivating Perseverance in Practice

You can cultivate perseverance in practice by:

- Knowing what you want. Being aware of your goals and visualising them so you can work harder, persevere more and carry on despite negativity.
- Knowing why you are doing the things you do.
- Loving the choices you've made so you can be motivated enough to overcome challenges.
- Embracing the fear of failure.
- Ignoring those who criticise you.

Resilience and perseverance in your personal life are also important to help you:

- Improve your academic achievement and learning.
- Reduce your chance of becoming dependent on drugs or alcohol and reduces your risk-taking behaviours.
- Increase your involvement in family and community activities.
- Improve your physical well-being.

> *"Stand up straight and realise who you are, that you tower over your circumstances."*
> – Maya Angelou

Find your path with confidence,

Cheryl Strickland

About the Author

Cheryl Strickland is a wellness coach, helping clients make positive and lasting changes to their health. Cheryl guides clients through the process of creating a vision for their health and well-being, developing healthy mindset and habits, and encouraging them every step of the way until they accomplish their goals.

As an integrative wellness coach, Cheryl views health and wellness from a holistic perspective, working with the whole person to thrive mentally, physically and spiritually.

Cheryl meets with clients in person or through online coaching sessions. Working together with her clients, Cheryl conducts health assessments and develops personalised plans to gain optimal health and well-being. The step-by-step plans help clients with goals such as:

- Stress management.
- Prioritising self-care.
- Maintaining a positive and healthy mindset.
- Balancing wellness and a busy schedule.
- Healthy eating.
- And much more.

Wellness by Cheryl Coaching

Website: https://coachingbycheryl.com

Email: wellnessbycheryl@gmail.com

Facebook: https://www.facebook.com/wellnessbycheryl/

Instagram: https://www.instagram.com/wellnesscoachcheryl/

LinkedIn: https://www.linkedin.com/coachingbycheryl/

Pinterest: https://pinterest.com/wellnessbycheryl/

Twitter: https://www.twitter.com/aromatherapygal/

Dedication

To my dearest aunt, Eda Davies, who inspired me with her talents and belief that a woman can achieve whatever she wants in her career.

Chapter Thirteen

Leading Well From Within
by Suzanne Duncan

Author, Mindset and Behavioural Coach, Australia

"Any journey of transformation begins with leading well from within."
– Suzanne Duncan

I'm an identical twin. My father is one, too! My twin sister and I grew up together in Canberra, Kalgoorlie, then Melbourne in Australia. My father is a geologist and met my mother when she was working at the same university. She came to Australia from Ireland via England at the age of nineteen with her suitcase, knowing no one. Hard to even contemplate doing that these days!

Our family moved around as was required of Dad's job. My sister and I attended different schools with each move, which meant that we were each other's best friend. Friends came and went.

So, we were constantly adjusting and adapting. Being introverts sometimes made it challenging.

Perhaps the fact that we were always moving gave me the ability to accept and manage change later. We certainly relied on and were there for each other. Being able to share and talk about how I was feeling and let things out was such a gift. I will always be grateful for my sister who gets me on the deepest level.

Family life growing up was about socialising with my parents' friends and getting to know the children of those friends. Dad's company had regular Christmas gatherings, and everyone kept in touch, even when people moved interstate.

One such family, ended up being my in-laws! And it all happened when they returned to Melbourne and visited us with their son James.

I was in my late twenties and had been in a long-term relationship that ended. James was looking for a new flat mate. So, I moved in. There was a spark right from the beginning, which grew as the months went on, and we eventually became lifelong partners … or that's what I thought we'd be when I said, "I do."

Our early years were full of adventure, interstate travel every Christmas to visit family, an overseas trip to join James in Bangkok when he was there for work, and keeping fit while enjoying an inner-city lifestyle.

Our first child was born in 2001, followed by two more in 2003 and 2005. We moved to an outer suburb and started getting to know other families in the area.

We dreamed of a long and fulfilling life together. How life can change …

James was a general manager and travelled extensively all over the world. His work colleagues and friends adored him. He was such a competent, thoughtful, warm and friendly man.

I was a stay-at-home mum looking after our precious children. It felt lonely at times and I had postnatal depression after our first child was born as motherhood changed everything. Gone were the days of working in medical research and the medical diagnostics industry. I was home twenty-four seven. My identity and my routine, or total lack of it, disappeared and it took time and tears to adjust.

It was challenging! I wasn't getting much sleep and running on empty, but we got through somehow. Our children were our focus and we had each other.

When our youngest was three years old, James was diagnosed with terminal bowel cancer. I remember sitting on our bed and he fell to the ground, weighed down by his prognosis. He sobbed and sobbed and was so upset with himself for overlooking his health and the impact it was now going to have on everything. He kept repeating to me that he felt like such an idiot. All I could do was to comfort and cry with him.

Unfortunately, his job and our family had been his focus. He'd neglected his health and was about to heartbreakingly pay the price.

I cared for him for two and a half years, existing in a fog of disbelief. When such an immense shock hit, it took us time to accept. My children and how they were coping took my attention, and James and his well-being was always my priority.

I wanted someone to come and rescue us. To make it all better. I wanted to spend the rest of my life with James. It was like we were moving towards a chasm and there was nothing we could do. It was getting closer and closer and we were all going to tumble over.

In the early days, he continued to work, and we were hopeful of remission. We kept busy, and while it was harrowing, it also brought us even closer together.

Relentlessly, the cancer progressed, and James turned his energy to setting his affairs in order and organising his memorial service. He chose the music, invited friends to give speeches and wanted to display a self-portrait painted by his mother.

During chemotherapy, he painstakingly wrote a journal of his life story for our children to read when they were older. He wanted them to know their Dad. To read in his own words about his life and who he was.

Here is an extract:

"Today I kissed you all goodbye and headed off on a trip to Thailand. I've finally bought this book and began to put down my thoughts for you to read if you are feeling sad or you just miss me. I want to tell you stories about myself and Mum and remind you of the great times we had together. I want to tell you all the things that I wanted to tell you as you get older, but I won't have the chance to say. Most of all I want you to know that you had a Dad who loved you deeply. As I started to write these thoughts Lachie is 8, Bella is 6 and Jess is almost 4. You are Mummy and my little treasures, and we talk every day about how lucky we have been as parents. I will eventually write to you about my illness. For now, I want to start by telling who your Dad is. So, let's start ..."

We watched him slowly decline and deal with unbearable pain. I remember after a bowel operation, we were travelling home, and he was in excruciating pain. At a railway crossing, he leapt out of the car and screamed and screamed. He was in so much pain. I was horrified to see him so debilitated. We drove home as he writhed in agony.

During the last six months, James wanted to be cared for at home. A palliative care nurse was assigned and visited regularly. She also offered advice to me as his primary caregiver.

On his last weekend, he came to watch our son play soccer. He sat with his parents, who had arrived from interstate several weeks earlier. James was gaunt and skeletal. He'd vomited up brown fluid earlier in the day. A doctor friend said, "He hasn't got much longer now."

Later that day, we sat on the bed. He held my hand and said, "Just keep on smiling, you'll be ok." My mum remembers our youngest daughter lying on the bed beside him, while he stroked her hands and chatted. His facial expression conveyed so much sorrow and regret that he wasn't going to live to see her grow.

Some friends visited. James wondered what to say to them. He was starting to lose oxygen to his brain. During the last two nights, he would cry out in his slept saying, "No, no." I couldn't sleep, helpless and unable to ease his suffering.

On his last night, his mum slept on a mattress near his bed. At about five in the morning, we called his dad, saying that he needed to be here. We were in the kitchen when his dad arrived. His mum went to check on James. We heard an anguished cry as she ran back to us, crying, "Suze, Suze, he's gone." She was understandably inconsolable. James died at six-thirty on a Monday morning in June 2011.

Our children, who were four, seven and nine years old, were asleep. We woke them and told them that Daddy had died and our friends were going to look after them until a bit later.

The palliative care nurse came and asked me to help prepare James' body for the undertakers. Brown fluid had gushed out of his mouth and was trickling over the bed. We cut off his pyjamas, moved him away from the soiled bedding and put everything in bags.

We cleaned and dressed him in the clothes he'd chosen to be cremated in, his body now ready for removal. To look at, touch and move a dead body that used to be my beloved husband and see him carried out in a body bag – it was harrowing.

Later that morning, our children came home. My youngest daughter asked my mum, "Where is Daddy?" and she was told that some people were taking care of him. She asked, "Can we ring him?" but was told, "No, that wasn't possible."

James was forty-four years old. I shattered into a million pieces.

James had been my rock, and I had been his. Now there was a vast emptiness. I was living on autopilot. Getting up, looking after my children, going to work, coming home, going to bed. Repeat. Day after day while coping with grief and no family support in Melbourne. I made the decision to stay in Melbourne for my children to have stability in their lives. We knew people here and I thought that would help.

Five years later a friend gave me a ticket to *Date with Destiny*, a Tony Robbins event. I had no idea what to expect. It was an amazing experience, and during a healing meditation I released my grief. I was deeply immersed. The deeper I went, the lighter I felt. I was happy, even though tears streamed down my face. Images of James floated around my mind. Filled with love that he had been in our lives, that we had three beautiful children together and we'd had those years creating a life together; I felt overwhelming gratitude and joy. Those years with him were precious, and they shine on.

That's not to say that I don't feel sad when special anniversaries come up or when my teens reach their milestones. There will always be residual sadness no matter how much I move on from the past.

What I still faced, though, was the solo journey and finding the strength to keep on keeping on.

I had to find myself again. Grief had defined me for five years and my focus was my children and meeting their needs. I barely focused on what I needed and pursued things without much thought. They were simply things to do or buy.

I wasted a lot of time and money chasing them. Hoping they would bring meaning and fulfilment to my life. However, all the material stuff I feathered my nest with is just stuff.

How lost and aimless I unconsciously was. I was placing so much emphasis on external things to prop me up. To make me feel good. To rescue me from feeling empty.

I realised that I'd replaced my grief with shiny object syndrome. The rush of new things was addictive but superficial. And I had to rescue myself.

I could rescue myself! No one was coming to rescue me. No knight in shining armour! I wanted to be my own inspiration. Was I my own role model? There was no vision for the future other than my teens and seeing them grow into independent young adults.

And I could find the strength within, to focus on making a difference. I had to focus on myself first. I had to explore more of what makes me, me. A journey within.

This was my turning point. This is what changed my life. When I thought about James and the experience of him losing his life, someone who so desperately wanted to live, I reassessed my own life. Life is short! And I wanted to make the most of it.

I started to look at people, issues and problems differently. How much time was wasted sweating the small stuff! How precious life is. Scary at times? Yes. Hard at times? Yes. But with awareness, insight and compassion for where I was, I began.

Once I realised that I am the only one who can change my life, things started happening.

I have all the resources within. I just needed to reconnect the pieces like a giant jigsaw puzzle. I loved coaching and transformation, so I started with myself, studying and learning all I could.

I asked myself why was I doing this? For what purpose did I want this? To be the best possible version of myself, not only for myself, but also for my teens who stood beside me. To not settle, to explore further and find out just how far I can learn, grow, evolve and inspire others to do the same.

What did I need to change? What did I need to prioritise? I examined my life. What was serving me in a functional way, what was dysfunctional and needed to be released?

How was I going to move forward? What rituals was I adopting to get me to where I wanted to be? Consistency was key and I honoured my mind, body and soul with nourishing habits that gave me energy and calm and enabled me to thrive.

Who was I surrounding myself with? Who was my role model? The more inspiring and further along in their personal development journey, the more positive a role model they were.

When I truly understood this, my intention for each day changed. My attention focused on moving forward.

Success starts with that journey within. It's a personal thing and for me it was finally understanding what lit up inside me, what I was passionate about and wanted to pursue, helping others get to know who they are on the deepest level.

And the ripple effects began from there. In all areas of life from health and wealth, to relationships and career. My teens are shining too, enjoying life and pursuing what they love.

My business Discovery Within helps professionals change their lives to create a life by design, to find focus and clarity to live abundant lives through a two-month STEMM process – Success, Taking Stock, Evolution, Momentum, Maintenance.

I wrote a book for single parents to inspire them, available in thirty bookshops in Australia and New Zealand. Ten percent of the proceeds go to the Shaun Miller Foundation, a charity for congenital heart disease research. This led to a speaking engagement at a fundraising event.

I've been interviewed on podcasts, had articles published globally, been on the cover of an international women's magazine and been invited onto local radio to talk about how to cope and manage change.

And this all started with changing myself and being ok with the ups and downs.

Here are some of my biggest learnings and I hope they inspire you because you can do anything you set your mind to!

1. You have infinite resources within. Rediscover them and use them to elevate your life.
2. No matter what change comes in life, there is always a way to move on.
3. Have self-compassion. You've been doing the best you can.
4. Momentum comes through movement. A little step forward is better than none.
5. Seek support. Life is too short to live a life of quiet desperation. And you are worth it. You matter.

"Be your own leader. Create your own ripples!"
– Suzanne Duncan

All the best,

Suzanne Duncan

About the Author

Suzanne Duncan is an author and mindset and behavioural coach.

She founded her business, Discovery Within, in 2016, where she runs coaching programmes and behavioural profiling assessments.

Suzanne insightfully guided me in a direction I wasn't expecting. This meant Suzanne was able to create awareness around my real problem – a lack of self-acceptance, which was impacting on my clarity and direction.
– Sue Stevenson.

She is the author of *All by Myself & Rocking It! How to be Successful at Single Parenting.*

Suzanne is also the creator of the STEMM method for professionals who want to lead a life by design with clarity, focus and motivation without the feelings of overwhelm or stress to achieve more fulfilment, abundance and better relationships.

Discovery Within

Website: https://discoverywithin.com.au/
Email: suzanne@discoverywithin.com.au
Facebook: https://www.facebook.com/suzanne.duncan.982/
Instagram: https://www.instagram.com/suzanneduncan_/
LinkedIn: https://www.linkedin.com/in/suzannerduncan/

Dedication

To my teenagers, Lachie, Bella and Jessie, for being themselves as we learn, grow and evolve together to be all that we can be. I love you always.

And to my late husband James, your memory shines on.

Chapter Fourteen

Becoming love
by Kerry Cleopatra

Womens Sacred & Soul Coach, Healer and Mentor, Founder of 'The Beautiful Place', Australia

*"Where there is love, there is no space for fear …
imagine you, imagine a world … with so much love!"*
– Kerry Cleopatra

To get to the "becoming love" bit – to understanding and truly becoming – we need to understand and unstitch a few things first. I trust you've already begun before now and transformed much already! Bear with me, as I intend to inspire the next whole and Divine expression and bare beauty of you – as best I can within this moment. We may need to turn upside down and slightly inside out, and let's dare to be more deeply honest than ever before, and it is ok to be messy where needed!

It can feel a bit much sometimes – the ignorance, the awakeness, the in-betweenness we're navigating. And to add to the challenge of working our stuff out – the current speed of light has many of our heads spinning! It can feel that just when we get to a good place or have enough of an aha moment to put the old stuff behind us, the moon does another cycle, the season does its thing and the world throws a tool box at us (no longer a simple spanner!).

So, how the heck do we stay "in love" with ourselves? In some cases, how do we even know what it really is!? And is self-love enough? Is it the answer?

Firstly, let's clarify the difference between self-love and being love! I feel self-love is something we seem to work at – the part that is the effort toward feeling love. Being love is when it is no longer an effort – it is your natural state and way of being. Being love is a realisation that you are the love.

I offer you five new paradigms to consider (trust your gut, you will know if you align, even if you don't yet fully understand). Really – they may be both principles and paradigm shifts, as we move towards changing our mind, perception and thoughts to shape our reality more on our own terms. Let's begin with a biggie:

1. The Purpose of Self-Love Is to Become Love

Sounds simple, and it is, except we can be complicated, emotional human beings! To begin with, let's identify some of what is and is not self-love:

Self-love is a choice to care for yourself, and it's often a work in progress that requires some focus and commitment. According to some dictionaries, self-love is "love of self, such as an appreciation of one's own worth or value." Genuine self-love is not selfish, even though it requires a genuine commitment to self. To be clear, self-love is not harming or blaming others in the rush to get the love of yourself in order. It is not necessary to spend great amounts of time or money to prove your love and commitment either. Although treating yourself can be a beautiful thing, self-love need not be done in big moments with big but often inconsistent or unsustainable gestures. In fact, it need not be thought of as a dramatic effort at all.

I have discovered the most joy in simply living and breathing self-love as a daily awareness. Being aware of your simple self-kind actions can help your mind recognise the love within you. Even brushing your teeth is an act of self- love and care. It can be that simple – being aware of what you do for yourself, rather than berating yourself for where you think you miss or fail. What you focus on grows – *focus on recognising simple daily love!*

Breathe for a moment (now's a good time for a simple pause). What have you done for yourself lately? Just picking up a book like this to grow and nourish yourself, seeking answers (or are you actually remembering what you already align with!). You could add this to your self-love recognition! What else did you do? Shower, stretch, eat with thought, walk and appreciate some trees, smile in the mirror for just a moment or longer, hold some gratitude, offer yourself compassion?

I trust that you're getting the idea for simple, daily acts and recognition to grow your self- love and your awareness, awakening the actual undying love that is within you – this is who you are! Undying, no matter the darkest moments. Your light is eternal – that I promise.

Self-love is a process – being present and patient gives vital nourishment for the cause! It's ok, no matter where you are right now. You are who you have become, now you can become who you wish to.

Self-love is a matter of unravelling some of what was taught and indoctrinated, followed by the reprogramming that feels better for you. It's not to beat yourself or others up. It is simply to recognise, using a kind and very honest observation. Save judgement for more positive use such as making decisions, rather than the time-wasting abuse of yourself or others (unless of course you have reason to hang out with pain for a little longer).

So, there are a few "nots" – now the way forward. It's fine to draw a line in the sand as each day is a new opportunity. *As we know better, we can do better* and *from little things big things grow* (my favourite reminder/mantra as I trek my own transformations).

2. Living Your Soul's Desire Is Living Your Authentic Self

Here are some self-enquiry prompts – I invite you to grab pen and paper, or just sit and ponder:

Who do you want to be now? What is burning within you to come forward? Who do you really want to be (dig deeper again)? What feels most like your heart and soul? How do you want to feel – in general, in daily life, in life reflections, in contemplating the legacy you leave for your loved ones and fellow humans? What is your footprint, dear soul? Is it alongside many other footprints that walk a path you align with and would like to contribute? Is it a pathway that you must forge anew? Is it enough of a desire that life no longer makes sense to walk without this reason and direction?

Perhaps it is, and if it is not yet, fear not. You may simply have weight, blocks or burdens to unravel, to release, so that you may breathe deeply and lightly again, allowing the space for your "in-spirit-ation" to glow brightly!

This is not a race, although we've been titled the human race. I'd like to shift this title to "our humans being". None the less, the idea is that we stop racing and start being. Being present, being real, being ourselves – and being brave enough to do so. A t least the bravery is needed only until the compulsion replaces the bravery. This is when the compulsion to be who you are becomes non- negotiable. The transformation is truly in action as it hurts more to live any other way than yours!

There is some time and space necessary for the unravelling of the old wounds and stories, letting go of the blaming, grief, victim-ness, perceptions and judgements, allowing us expansion, understanding and self-response-ability. At the same time, forward movement continues, sometimes slowly, sometimes in great leaps!

Some ways to support the loving expansion of yourself: read good material, write your stuff "out", speak and listen with good people who help spark your light even brighter, immerse yourself in healing and living at the same time. Make spaces within you, allow more light from within to glow outwards and attract wonderful supportive circumstances for what it is you now wish to create and attract. Create space to hear your soul speak. Invest what is needed for your greatest self to emerge – life is too short for living less than your burning desires!

We can learn more by listening within. Self-enquiry and good questions can clear clutter and allow space for your wisdom to spill out beautifully and candidly. Clarity is powerful and spacious! So, no matter the stage of your personal awareness and transformation, it is helpful to do check-ins with your personal enquiries. Revisit them and rewrite your answers as you evolve. Nothing is set in concrete – you are free to change your mind and evolve accordingly!

You are welcome to use some of the questions I have suggested here. There are further tools available on my website, listed at the end of this chapter. I regularly check in with my heart and soul and have dedicated a writing book just for this purpose. I like a blank A3 book so that I am unlimited in my expressions of self-enquiry. Find your way to write for clarity – it is so useful and powerful to get it all out of your head and see what comes.

Here's a writing tip: sit somewhere you feel comfy in. It could be the back lawn on a warm day, a big tree space, yoga mat, comfy couch or your favourite cafe. Clear your mind, attachments and expectations by holding that very intention, breathe three times to let go, then allow the space for what will come. This way you are more likely to allow the soul a say!

A little tip: If you cannot still the mind enough to let go and listen, then empty some "stuff" out first by simply free writing and getting it out! No judgements necessary, you're just releasing. For this purpose, do your best to stay out of the hooks of your own stories, let go, breathe and write that stuff out. Cry, wail, breathe – you're ok beautiful, perfect soul.

3. You Are Not Failing, You Are Expanding

Sometimes when you find yourself revisiting old stuff – or new stuff keeps coming up – it can feel like you're not getting anywhere, or even failing (that was my nemesis story – I'm a failure! Pfft!). If you can relate, here's the lowdown on this one: it's simply not true! We don't call a child a failure for falling twenty times before they master riding a bike. We encourage and love them. Let's be kinder as we are learning to ride the waves of life! Something I realised in my own growth spirals is that I keep expanding my vision and beliefs. Therefore, I am always learning the next lesson or clearing old stuff that would otherwise hold me back. I am not failing, I am simply expanding further.

Feel free to consider that option of belief. I find that it works for me, and my clients have shifted some of their self-defeating and self-critical ways, too! This belief is much more powerful for loving, encouraging and supporting yourself well. We are always changing and evolving (even with a stagnant pond, there is change none the less!). Change is inevitable.

4. It Is Not Happening to You, It Is Happening for You

Your body supports you every step of the way (not always easy to trust in this one, I understand!) When the body aches, or the circumstance slaps you in the face, is it happening to you, or for you? Which is the empowering option? I choose "for you". Ponder that for a moment if you need. There's nothing more empowering than changing any remnant victim status for good.

When your body is ill, why not hear and heed its message. What an opportunity! If an accident happens, why not see what you can learn from it, what it might be telling you. When a relationship ends or when you lose a loved one (not easy, I know!), what does it allow you to recognise, let go of, shift, change and strengthen within you? Life and death are part of existence and nature. To honour your feelings, go through and expand amongst it all – that is the opportunity we all have should we choose. Honouring your emotions (energy in motion) is important – just be aware of the tipping point when we stay too long and create further pain.

I choose to live a magical life, one filled with all the messages, answers and opportunities, one that supports my deepest and dearest desires. I am human amongst it all and allow myself my aching, grief, pain and misery when needed. I just don't stay too long and return to my faith in the wisdom of life. It is not always easy but it is easier than staying in anger and resistance!

Because of my acceptance and faith in life, the ebb and flow of life do not fully consume or dictate my experience anymore. My heart and soul do that! It wasn't always like that for me. I wanted to leave this planet countless times. I'm glad to be here now! What do you want for you now? Would you like love to be who you are and how you feel – not a passing moment so rare that it hardly seems worth it?

It takes One. Single. Shift.

5. Love Is Who You Are!

This is the truth! Recognise your true innate self!

Anytime, you are welcome to align with this truth. Accept all that is, change what you wish to, keep moving with faith in yourself and this life you absolutely chose Divine one!

Ask of yourself what your heart truly desires, do whatever it takes to move toward this and with this in daily life, have patience and grace

– for the processes of transformation do not move necessarily as we expect. They do however move for your highest good. Sometimes we do need to dig up some old stuff that we thought we were done with.

If you've raised your bar or desires and you are committed to them, life will give you whatever you need to shift old stuff that would otherwise hold you back. Hence, you're not failing, you are raising, expanding and evolving – how exciting! Where is your body telling you stuff, your work circumstances, relationships, etc? What is right before your eyes? Where are things no longer feeling right for you? You might just need a little tweaking to be in your flow of desires, or like I was, you may need a big, fat, overwhelming overhaul, again!

I offer you some good "remembering" that have served me, and may serve you now:

Remember – *from little things big things grow.* Start getting clear first, metaphorically and literally. Then your decision- making and direction is more likely to be taking you to your full heart's desires.

Remember – *you are not alone.* I was a master at feeling alone and with the self-fulfilling prophecy from what I believed of myself, that I was not worth anything, etc. – blaaaak! What a lie I believed! Surround yourself with good-hearted people who allow and inspire you further to be yourself!

Remember – *we are all in this together*. It takes a world of people to create breakdowns in society, communities, families and individuals. Yes, a world of people! And together we can create a beautiful, loving, amazing world with great love, learning and living!

Remember – *your commitment to self-love can be simple*. It can be every day acts of awareness, gratitude and kindness in the simple things.

Remember – *through the art of self-love we become the love!* We always were and we still are. We are just shedding the "stuff" that has blocked our remembering that we are actually Divine creations of, and from, love. And we can feel that love within and for ourselves, always.

Remember – *being love is peaceful.* If you fall off the peace train, don't worry – it is your truth, so you will always return to it. Think of

Dorothy from the Wizard of Oz – there's no place like home. All you need to do is tap into your remembering!

> *"You are unlimited, Divine love, capable of anything you set your heart's desire to.*
> *Now go choose beautiful – align and allow!"*
> – Kerry Cleopatra

My love sees and appreciates you.

Much love, always,

Kerry Cleopatra

About the Author

Bringing through the authentic feminine is Kerry's natural love! Her approach is a collaborative of Earth wisdom and Divine awakening with healing and soul reconciliation. Kerry's ability to blend the esoteric with good, honest, intelligent science is unique – she is loved for her ability to bridge the gap between the intuitive and physical – in a grounded, understandable (often humourous), practical way!

Through her love of soul work, "Kerry Cleopatra" was born. As a coach, mentor and healer, Kerry dedicates space to support women to live their soul driven life – for success on their own terms! Kerry also holds certification in Health and Nutrition Coaching, Life coaching, Human Biology, Micro-biology and Chemistry, amongst growing herself through inspiring workshops.

With passion for truth, in 2007 Kerry founded "eKoo" – blending energy and organics to make artisan skincare, oils and teas – award winning & nurturing thousands! To this day she is still hands on, creating with love and joy!

In 2020, Kerry founded "The Beautiful Place" – an artisan and heart space in the Barossa Valley, South Australia – with the vision "to inspire the beautiful place within us all!" Truly beautiful!

Kerry currently lives in the Barossa – and is embracing her own 50s transition! She cherishes her time with family and friends – particularly enamoured with her gorgeous grandgirls! In between imagining, making, teaching and playing, Kerry is a planet and truth loving activist. She is a sensitive soul that leads passionately – inspiring us to live our own authentic adventures to!

Many of the principles and paradigms shared here are expanded on the website. Kerry would love to connect with you further and invite you to visit – online or in person. Enjoy more simple tools to assist your Divine expansion!

Kerry Cleopatra

Website: www.kerrycleopatra.com, www.thebeautifulplace.com.au
Email: kerry@kerrycleopatra.com
Facebook: www.facebook.com/kerry.cleopatra.3
Instagram: https://www.instagram.com/kerrycleopatra

Dedication

To those who cannot not love us all the time, allowing us to dig deeper than we like, to become more of who we truly are, to become the love we once sought outside of ourself.

To you reading this and showing up again and again – fossicking with me – persisting with us all – as we dig and sift in the depths, awakening to the heavenly truths of our very beings. Thank you beautiful one! Together – We. Are. Love.

Chapter Fifteen

Empowerment – The Greatest Strength Comes From Within

by Martin Probst

Award-Winning Learning Professional, Facilitator, Speaker & Leadership Coach, Australia

"Leadership is about guidance to a clear vision, unlocking true potential and creating excellence as a result of heightened awareness, accountability and inspiring actions."
– Martin Probst

When I grew up in rural Switzerland (in a village of around 250 people), as the youngest in a traditional Swiss family setting, the world seemed to be simple and my path destined and clearly laid out. That, however, didn't take into account my desire to travel and see the world, my longing for spending time on a cruise ship, and my dream of palm trees in my backyard. These deep-seated desires might have been one of the unconscious reasons why I chose to become a chef.

Little did I know back then that this profession is not all globetrotting glory. In fact, it brought along gruelling 16-hour workdays, rigid kitchen hierarchy and enormous sacrifices. It was the end of playing my beloved team sport, spending public holidays such as Christmas with my family and friends, and enjoying a healthy work-life balance.

Regardless of the long hours, the incredible dedication to the job and the endless devotion to giving my absolute best, I still felt unfulfilled.

In fact, I felt empty and miserable. I did not realise back then that I was trying to please everybody – except myself. Countless times I was collapsing on the couch after a double shift and was still telling myself that I should have done better and more. I constantly told myself that my work was not perfect, and that my outcomes (which ultimately meant I myself) was not good enough.

Life Is Too Short to Burn the Midnight Oil – When Is Enough, Enough?

You are probably well aware that Switzerland is the land of perfectionism and precision; just think about Swiss watches, Swiss chocolate and of course Roger Federer! To fit in and achieve a sense of acceptance and belonging, I instinctively allowed the "Swiss way" to condition me to aim for perfectionism, not realising that perfectionism does not exist in that sense.

Today, I firmly believe that we are all perfect in our own way, with all our flaws and shortcomings, striving to create a better version of ourselves every single day; sometimes successfully, sometimes not. But, hey, that makes us human, doesn't it? Ultimately, who we are right now is a wonderful thing and creates an important feeling of acceptance of ourselves and others.

I grew up to live my life "at effect". This means that I reacted to everybody and everything around me, rather than causing things to happen and being in control of my life. I did not understand when enough is enough; I was always ready to be the rescuer, to step up to the plate and to go above and beyond everyone else's expectations (just not those of my own). I did not know who I truly was and what I stood for; I was lost while pursuing a career and business success that I believed would give me what I was looking for in life.

Even when I reached the top of the "food chain" and became Chef de cuisine, or head chef, achieving my lifelong goal of travelling international waters and appearing on national television, I still felt empty and constantly sought external approval from customers, employees, family members, friends and many others around me.

In 2001, I even migrated to Australia on the other side of the planet, not realising that wherever I went, I took myself with me. This reminds me of a quote from Tony Robbins, who rightfully said:

> *"Success without fulfilment is the ultimate failure."*

That is exactly how I felt when I hit rock bottom.

Mindset Moments – Letting Go of the Excuses

Looking back to the first three decades of my life, what stands out to me is my mindset of being "at effect" – reacting rather than acting, seeking approval rather than feeling empowered. I was filled with fear and doubts; I felt trapped in my career seeing myself as "only a chef". During that time, I was full of excuses and was blaming people around me and the environment for my misery and the depressing situation.

All this became quite evident throughout my journey of writing my first book. For years, I had talked up the fact that I was going to write a book (which was quite an achievement back in Switzerland, where the society consists of brilliant but mediocre individuals). Being a famous author-in-the-making certainly made me feel significant and good about myself. I would talk about it for hours with my family and friends, and anybody else who was willing to listen.

But it was just that: a lot of talk, and no action or outcome. The excuses kept coming: "I was too busy with my current job", "It just was not the right time to get started", "I didn't have enough support from those around me". You name the excuses, I had them all.

Then one day came the realisation, not without a lot of persistence and help of my friends who held me accountable and kept asking about the progress of my book. I felt like a fraud because I was simply talking and not delivering. I was ashamed as I realised that I did not walk the talk. I realised that the buck stopped with me.

> *"You can either have excuses or results, but you can't have both."*
> *– Arnold Schwarzenegger*

So, I had to make a decision. I realised that I had to shift my focus and adopt more empowering thoughts and a positive vocabulary to take control of my life. This is when I moved from a dependent mindset of

"What's out there has to change first" to an independent mindset of *"What changes can I make to influence what's out there"*.

Interestingly enough, after this incredible paradigm shift, the decision was actually pretty simple. I truly understood and felt in my entire being that **empowerment comes from within.** It is crucial to understand that our mindset has an enormous impact on how resourceful we are or can become.

I created clarity for myself around what I stand for, what my purpose is on this planet and the life I live, what my values are, and first and foremost to accept myself for who I am. Ultimately, we are all value-fulfilling machines and we must decide whether we are fulfilling our own purpose, vision and values (living true to ourselves) or try to live somebody else's life, based on their values, beliefs and expectations (being conditioned by others).

I learned to be my authentic self, which makes sense when you think about it; because everybody else is already taken.

Better Times Might Be Right Now – You Just Need to See It

We often feel compelled to accommodate or fulfil other people's dreams, and we forget how to look after ourselves and to live a life full of confidence and authenticity.

The moment I decided to break free from the conditioning of my upbringing and position myself in a way that I could live a genuine and fulfilling life was when the transformation started for me on a personal level.

The real transformation in my business, however, was when I started to move from an independent and empowering mindset to a collaborative mindset. As Helen Keller, beautifully said:

> *"Alone we can do so little, together we can do so much."*

This new passion for collaboration has provided me with countless great opportunities that I never would have imagined myself taking before I switched perspectives. Once I adopted this collaborative mindset with the help of my beautiful wife Gerda, who has been my life partner of over twenty years and is also my business partner, my family, my community and network, as well as the help of other companies, my business ultimately skyrocketed.

The fear of going back to a limiting and unsatisfying state of dependence held me back for a long time. I thought that collaborating with others meant exposing my vulnerabilities and risking my well-earned success. But it's really not! Collaboration by definition is:

> *"Independent individuals and/or companies working together by appreciating their different skillsets and leveraging from each other's strengths."*

This is when 1 + 1 = 3 or more. As Aristotle duly noted a long time ago:

> *"The whole is greater than the sum of the parts."*

A beautiful example of the incredible benefits of collaboration comes from Mother Nature. Wildlife scientists have conducted extensive studies to determine why geese and other migratory birds always fly in a distinctive V-formation. They found some fascinating results:

Firstly, when geese fly together in this pattern, each member of the flock provides additional lift and reduce air resistance to those behind them. As a consequence, it is estimated that the entire flock can fly about 70% further with the same energy than if every goose were to fly alone.

Secondly, birds flying in a V-formation rotate leadership because of the additional energy that is required of the bird flying at the front. When the leading bird gets tired, it moves to the back of the formation with the lightest resistance, and a different bird takes on the leadership position.

Another interesting fact is that geese help and support each other. If one goose becomes ill or injured, for example, and as a consequence drops out of the V-structure, two other geese will also leave the formation and remain with their weakened friend. They fly alongside and protect the injured goose from predators until it can fly again or dies.

I did it! – Start to Live Your Life by Design, Not by Default

My life has undergone an incredible transformation in the past few years. This can be attributed to my mindset shift; from first unconsciously living a very dependent life, to then consciously living a very independent life, to ultimately position ourselves (as a family and as collaborators) in the best possible way to live a life on our own terms.

Through the work I do in my business, I had the honour of being awarded "Learning Professional of the Year" in 2019 by the Asia Pacific Institute for Learning & Performance, and our business, PROfound Leadership, was named "Highly-Commended Learning Provider of the Year" as well as being ranked in the "Top 10 Leadership Development Training/Coaching Companies in APAC 2020".

Our vision for the future is to empower organisations, teams and individuals with human-centred leadership strategies, so they can overcome the toughest challenges in today's busy and ever-changing environment, as well as positively transform their future and generations to come.

This is aligned with my values and gives me daily inspiration and energy to challenge the status quo and strive for the best, authentic version of myself that I can be.

I adopted a mindset that gave me the results I desired – and you can as well. I invite you to transform your life and business, so you too can say, "I did it!"

There is a lot of leading in learning, so please let me share some of my simple yet PROfound wisdoms with you. My small guide to big changes will help you to transform the life you have into the ultimate life you desire.

1. Have a strong vision and purpose – Clearly understand what positive impact you would like to have on this planet and what legacy you would like to leave behind. Dreams don't understand the language of limitations, so be bold!

2. Replace perfection with progress and a high-achiever mindset – Know when enough is enough and celebrate your successes, no matter how big or small they are. This will give you inspiration and a sense of achievement that will keep you going.

3. A negative mind will never give you a positive life – You have over 60,000 thoughts per day, so be kind to yourself. Make sure your thoughts are positive and nurturing to support you and move closer to your vision and purpose.

4. Move away from asking what is right or wrong, and ask yourself what is working for you and what's not – This mindset will assist you to move from conditioning to positioning.

5. You don't have to do everything yourself – It is a strength to ask for help and to collaborate with others.

6. Build honest relationships with yourself and others – Surround yourself with independent people. Create a strong foundation of trust with them to work together by contributing and sharing knowledge and resources for a greater outcome.

7. Cultivate a collaborative environment – Foster a supportive culture, where individuals know and understand that they matter, belong and can contribute to a common goal.

8. Self-development is better than self-sacrifice – Invest into your most important real estate, which is the one you have between your ears.

> *"Your journey to self-discovery and leadership starts here. Let's close the gap between where you are and where you want to be. This is a path worth pursuing, because you are worth it; you are lovable; and you are enough!"*
> – Martin Probst

Dare to make a difference!

Martin Probst
AWARD-WINNING
LEARNING PROFESSIONAL

About the Author

Martin Probst is an international author, award-winning learning professional, facilitator, speaker and leadership coach who lives in Melbourne, Australia.

Through his company, PROfound Leadership, Martin helps managers and leaders to empower themselves with skills of the future, so they can lead with confidence and positively impact the people around them through their actions and authentic leadership style.

His mission to maximise human potential to achieve peak performance in a supportive work environment has led him to:

- Work in different industries in six continents over 30 years.
- Be a certified learning facilitator (Institute for Learning & Performance) and other modalities.
- Design and deliver over 160 workshops and speaking engagements.
- Teach over 10 years in formal education.
- Facilitate over 1,000 hours of one-on-one coaching sessions.
- Author six Australian and international books, audio books and leadership journal.
- Be awarded "Learning Professional of the Year" at the 2019 Australian Learning Impact Award.
- His company being named "Highly-Commended Learning Provider of the Year" at the 2019 Australian Learning Impact Award.
- His company being ranked in the "Top 10 Leadership Development Training/Coaching Companies in APAC 2020".

Martin has directly impacted the lives of many managers in Australia and around the globe through his simple-yet-effective and solution-based leadership strategies, so they can successfully deal with the human aspects of the business.

His clients can't believe how simple and easy these strategies are to learn and apply, and what immediate and profound impact they have on their professional and personal lives:

> *"It blows my mind that Martin Probst can deliver that kind of mindset change in such a short period of time."*
> *– Kirsty Milligan, CEO & Entrepreneur*

Martin continuously publishes leadership articles on his PROfound Leadership blog, as well as on his LinkedIn profile. He has published several books, resources and a Leadership Journal, which are all available on his online shop. Martin has also published several online courses on leadership topics, the latest being "Confident Conflict Management".

PROfound Leadership

Website: https://profoundleadership.com.au
Email: martin@profoundleadership.com.au
Facebook: https://www.facebook.com/profoundleadership
Instagram: https://www.instagram.com/profoundlead/
LinkedIn Company: https://www.linkedin.com/company/profoundleadership/
LinkedIn Personal: https://www.linkedin.com/in/martinprobst/

Dedication

I feel a deep sense of gratitude for my amazing clients, with whom I have worked with over the years, for giving me great insights into human behaviours and teaching me how to ask the right questions, and to my supportive network that encouraged me along the way.

I am also deeply grateful to my beautiful wife and business partner, Gerda, who gave me "the push" to start to live life by design, not by default. And last but not least, my deepest gratitude goes to both of our delightful children for their ongoing support and for giving me purpose in life.

Chapter Sixteen

I Can Run
by Terri Tonkin
Author, Facilitator, Connector, Speaker and Coach, Australia

"Running is the greatest metaphor for life, because you get out of it what you put into it."
– Oprah Winfrey

I was born in Texas, a very small country town in South West Queensland. My dad's employment meant that we moved fairly regularly, about every two years. By the time I started school, I was living in my fourth town.

My parents had purchased the local dry-cleaning shop and went into business for themselves. I don't think they realised how much hard work it was going to be. My dad went to work in the early hours of the morning. My mum got my brothers and I ready for school, and then she went to work. When we got home from school, we all had chores to do, from cleaning school shoes, prepping vegetables for dinner, doing school homework or chopping wood.

When mum and dad returned home from the shop, we would have dinner and clean up, and sometimes, dad would return to the shop.

After a few years, they sold this shop, although mum continued to work there, as an employee. This meant that she would be on the road a couple of days each week, as she had to take the clothes to the Ipswich store to be cleaned and bring the cleaned ones back. Again, long days and lots of hours. Dad secured employment in

Brisbane, which meant that we saw him Friday night to Sunday night, as he would leave in the early hours of Monday morning to return to Brisbane. He was living with my maternal grandmother during this time.

That arrangement lasted a little over two years, before we purchased a house in Brisbane and the family moved, so we were all together again.

During my primary school years, I was involved in many different sports. I played vigoro, tennis and netball, and I particularly enjoyed swimming. I was a competitive member of the local swimming club for many years. When I graduated to high school, I was involved with softball and basketball. I continued playing basketball until I was in my thirties.

I started to develop problems with my knees, they would be painful after each game. I busted fingers many times. It was time to put the basketball away.

I had tried going to gyms a few times over the years, yet each time was short lived.

As I was approaching my fifties, a new gym opened in the next suburb. It was an all-female gym. It offered a variety of classes, personal training or if I chose to, I could go and do my own thing. I thought, why not, I can give this a try. The gym was on my way to work, and I could go either before or after.

I joined the gym in February, yet it did not open until May. In that short time, I had changed jobs, and I was working in the city. So much for being close by.

I was still able to attend either before or after work. The gym provided breakfast, so that was taken care of. I maintained that membership for almost twelve years, made many friends and still continue to exercise with some of them today.

At my new job, I met a young woman who loved to do triathlons. I thought to myself, how wonderful to be that fit, to be able to complete a course of swimming, bike riding and then running.

She used to train most days, sometimes two or three times a day. At lunch time, she would go for a run around the city. I asked if I could join her, but I wasn't a runner. She was grateful for the company so we would walk and talk. She slowly got me to do intervals of jogging and walking and then jogging for longer periods.

On our way back to work after one of these sessions, we passed a new boxing gym that had opened, offering a free trial for a week. We both decided that we would give it a go, and I loved it. Boxing was my new thing. I became a member of this gym as well.

I was going to get fit.

Some friends from my other gym were running once or twice a week. I decided to join them and give that a go too. I found that I really enjoyed the running time, as I was able to concentrate on myself. I went as fast or as slow as I felt I needed to. There were no expectations from the others in the group. At times I would turn around before them, so we would get back to our starting point at the same time.

We started to enter some smaller, competitive events. The International Women's Day 5 kilometres, the Mother's Day 8 kilometres. We had lots of fun, lots of laughter.

And then my triathlon friend suggested we do the Brisbane Bridge to Bridge, a 10-kilometre run. So many people said, if you can do 5 kilometres you can do 10 kilometres. At this point, I did start to question myself. Why?

But I did it.

I was changing. I was enjoying this running gig. Many people thought I was going a little crazy.

This is the woman who gave up basketball because her knees were giving her pain.

In September 2011, I made a decision. I decided I was going to do the 2012 Gold Coast Half Marathon, 21.1 kilometres. This was going to be my new challenge.

OMG! What was I thinking? I'm not a runner, I have never been. I was a swimmer and a team sports player.

Lots of things had to change. Lots and lots and lots of things. I had 10 months to prepare.

I was working full time in the city, which was a 40-minute train ride each way. I was still attending both gyms, and I was running two mornings a week with friends. Those runs would be around 5 to 6 kilometres, 30 to 40 minutes in duration. Not enough to get me to 21 kilometres.

I started reading running magazines. I was trying new techniques. I was doing interval training. I would do hill runs. I would run further. I would run longer. For someone who had always believed that they were not a runner, my perception was rapidly changing.

My training schedule became my new life. Mondays would be boxing and weights, Tuesdays were a run in the morning and boxing class at lunch time, Wednesdays were boxing, Thursdays were a run in the morning and boxing class at lunch time again, Fridays were stretch classes, Saturdays were my long run day, and Sundays were rest days.

It wasn't only my exercise routines that changed. My nutrition changed, as did my hydration. Food was my best fuel, to eat clean and green. Hydration was important, I had to maintain my fluid intake, even on days I wasn't running, and before, during and after a run. I had to trial different gels to make sure they didn't make me ill. I had to work out what would give me energy but be gentle on my stomach.

I had two pairs of running shoes, all the time. I purchased quality socks, so they didn't scrunch up in my shoes. I bought compression socks and leggings for longer runs. I had good quality material in my shirts so they didn't rub and chafe when running. There was so much to learn, and then to trial and tweaking.

Just prior to the event in 2012, my husband and I went for a short-stay holiday in Port Macquarie. I was still training. I went out one morning for a run, and on my return, my foot slipped off the edge of the path. Excruciating pain shot up my calf muscle. All I could think of was, *what have I done.*

Luckily, I got back to the apartment, alternated between hot and cold presses, massaged and found a local sport store and purchased some compression calf sleeves. It was so painful.

The day before we travelled to the Gold Coast, I was out playing with my grandson, I made a quick turn and the pain was back. I wasn't giving in. I was going to run this half marathon, or at least I would finish, even if it meant limping over the finish line. I had worked hard for 10 months. I was not letting this slip through my fingertips.

Early the next morning, around 5am, the runners were lining up to tackle the course. It was cold and dark. I was freezing. I was nervous. I was excited. I was proud to be on the starting line. My hubby and some friends were on the side, cheering for me.

The gun went off, and I was on my way. For this event, there was a time limit. If you weren't back within that time, the race was over. I hoped and prayed that didn't happen to me.

Five kilometres down, 10 kilometres down, turnaround at 12 kilometres, 15 kilometres done, 20 kilometres done, and the crowd is heavier, louder, cheering everyone on. I could finally see the finishing tunnel. Not long now. And yet, this seemed like the longest stretch of the whole run. Into the tunnel, and less than 500 metres to go. Nearly there, keep going, don't stop. Finally, I see the finish line. This is almost over. Keep going legs, don't give up, keep breathing. I am across the line, through to the assembly area.

I collapse with exhaustion and exhilaration. I am crying and laughing. I finished. At the age of 53, I had completed my first half marathon, 21.1 kilometres in 2 hours and 40 minutes.

I am a runner.

These are words I believed would never come from my mouth. And yet, they did.

I had also developed a somewhat competitive side. One member of the morning running group decided that he, too, would do the half marathon the next year. He was taller, stronger, took much bigger strides than me. He joined a running club and was determined to finish before me.

I decided that I wasn't going to let that happen. I stepped up my running programme. I engaged my personal trainer from the boxing gym to run with me in lieu of being in the gym. My biggest competitor was ME.

I got fitter. I got stronger. I was almost at optimal running weight. I was ready. I was excited.

In 2013, my running got better and faster, I was fitter and stronger in both body and mind, and I had grown so much. In that year, I ran my fastest 5 kilometres in 25 minutes, 8 kilometres in 47 minutes, 10 kilometres in 61 minutes, 14 kilometres in 91 minutes, and 21.1 kilometres in 2 hours and 28 minutes. Twelve minutes shaved from my first half marathon.

In 2014, I did it all again. So maybe the original thought that I was a little crazy had some truth to it.

I accomplished a personal best for the 21.1 kilometres run. I shaved a minute off my previous time.

How did I go from being a non-runner to half marathoner?

First and foremost, I had to believe in myself, set the challenge, and that I could achieve the goal.

I had to change my perceptions about so many aspects of my life. I had to see the result I was seeking and work towards it, literally step by step.

I committed to the challenge, set the goal, researched, drafted the plan and took the action I needed to. There was a lot of trial and tweaking. If I tried something that didn't work, I would adjust it until it did work.

I had the support of family and friends. Friends who would run with me, on the cold, early morning runs. Friends who ran with me on some of the shorter runs. Friends who came with me to the event, to support me and cheer me on. My husband would monitor my long runs, as I would give him the route I was taking and my anticipated running time. He would say, "If you aren't home by then, I will be out looking for you."

Members of both the gyms would check in with me, ask me about my training, ask how I was dealing with it all, and generally, being supportive of my goals. The personal trainers would ensure the weights and stretch training would complement my running training.

Mostly, it was my mindset. I believed that I had done the right training, I believed that I was capable, I believed in me.

A week after the first event, I was in Bali, completing a neuro linguistic programming (NLP) course. What a powerful combination of events. Competing in and completing a half marathon, and then learning NLP. Those events taught me more about myself and my mind than anything else I could imagine. The mind is a powerful thing.

In 2018, I completed a life coaching course and became a published author. In 2019 and 2020, I was a contributing author to four books.

In early 2019, I completed a three-day speakers' training, and stood and spoke in front of a roomful of people I had never met. In August of the same year, I stood on stage at IGNITE Brisbane and shared my tips to finding happiness.

Don't let age stop you. It really is only a number. If there are what seem to be obstacles in the way, find the way around or over them. We all can achieve the results or outcomes we are seeking with the right mindset.

My experiences have allowed me to grow as a person, as a mother, and as a grandmother. My children see me as someone that will give something a go, especially when I have never tried it before. My grandchildren see that age is not a barrier, and especially my granddaughters can see that women who put their mind and their passion into something can achieve it.

I have been married to my husband for over forty years. He is still my biggest supporter and best friend.

My running opened my mind to opportunities that I may not have even been aware of. By having the awareness of the power of the mind and how it can be so motivating, my world has changed.

I completed my coaching training, authored and contributed to a number of books, left my secure government job, started a business, been a speaker on stage and am loving life.

You too, can change your life.

Set a goal. Do your homework on what and who you need or don't need. Prepare the plan. Take the action. Have a great support system around you – engage personal and professional supports.

Enjoy every moment and learn from every moment.

> *"A muscle is like a car. If you want it to run well early in the morning, you have to warm it up."*
> – Florence Griffith Joyner

Be grateful. Appreciate what you have.

Cheers for now,

Terri Tonkin

About the Author

Terri is a published author (*My Time To Shine*; *Business Warriors – Taking Care of Working Women In The 21st Century*; *Change Makers*; *Forever Changed by Suicide*; *I Did It!*), speaker, facilitator for Women Embracing Business network and workshops, mentor and coach.

Terri is the face of Connect Within life coaching and is based in the northern suburbs of Brisbane. Her clients are heard, validated, acknowledged, encouraged and supported to find the solutions they are searching for.

Terri believes that every person has the capacity within them to create the life they choose to have. By assisting her clients to transition and transform, a ripple effect is created when they are able to empower others by paying it forward.

Terri aspires to inspire the people she meets, to reach their potential, as inspiration leads to motivation, and motivation leads to action, providing results.

Her life has been a journey of ups and downs, trials and tribulations, both personally and professionally. She is a life-long learner, seeks out new opportunities, is an avid reader and loves to travel.

Terri draws on her diverse skills developed through her experiences, numerous employment opportunities, and cultural awareness from the many locations in which she has lived.

If you want to reclaim your zest for life and your motivation to live your life by design, rather than by default, Terri will work with you to achieve your goals.

Happiness is a choice, and you can choose it every day.

Connect Within

Website: www.connectwithin.com.au

Facebook: https://www.facebook.com/connectwithinmindsetlifecoach/

Email: terri@connectwithin.com.au

LinkedIn: https://www.linkedin.com/in/terri-tonkin/

Dedication

To my husband Roger, who has supported me over many years with his encouragement to pursue whatever I set my mind to.

To my children and grandchildren, thank you for loving me and my crazy dreams.

Testimonials cont...

Suzanne's story takes you through every emotion. There is an instant connection with your heart as she describes connection, love, loss and life. It leaves you inspired, wanting more. I am so grateful to you for sharing your journey with us.

Liz Murray – Focus Strategist, Newcastle, Australia.

Suzanne, it was a privilege to share the roller-coaster of both joy and connection that genuine love holds with another human being and then the unexpected loss when it is taken from you. This is the gift you have from your experience and your compassion shines through.

Katherine Robertson – Leadership Transformation Coach, Torquay Australia.

Joslyn Gardiner

The difference that Joslyn can achieve in people's lives through hypnotherapy is tangible and significant. Joslyn is so truly dedicated to helping people become the best version of themselves on so many levels.

Suzi Manley – Owner Five Rope Business Connective Brisbane Australia

An insightful story of turning failures into success, never giving up when life turns on you! Joslyn, who once looked up to mentors for guidance has become a successful mentor in her own right and willingly offers guidance to others.

Paula Axam – Personal Trainer, Brisbane Australia

To be an effective coach you need both technique and personal experience. Joslyn's past makes her an authority on rising above challenges and reflects in the results she achieves in her business.

Maureen Hamilton – Life Coach, Brisbane Australia

Scotty Lawrence

Wow loved it Scott! You took me on a journey and showed me your soul. I love the fact that you are totally honest with ups and downs, your pain and conquests. Your path was created for you to be a leader... Thank you.

Col Barrow

It brought up a raw state for me where I could tell it had a lot of honesty and openness. I have felt alone in so many things in my life and this is just another example of how much we all go through that we are not alone. Truly inspiring.

Pete Gagliardo

This could be a movie. I loved going on this journey with Scott as he transformed from a caterpillar to a butterfly. I felt my heart strings being pulled with the values and lessons that he shared along the way. It made me feel like good about myself. Best thing I have read in a long time!

Darren Hillar

Sally Holden

Sally is an inspiration to me. She supported me through tough times in my life where I was burnt-out and exhausted and has helped me to restore my balance and enabled me to see a bright and adventurous future ahead.

Anna Saunders – Leadership Mentor, Mount Keira, Australia.

When you work with Sally, you quickly realise that she brings ALL of herself. Her communication has an authenticity and heart that is incredibly rare and makes you feel deeply at ease.

Kate Wiggs – Family Therapist, London, UK

Sally is courageous and a life learner. She always asks herself and her clients great thought-provoking questions that inspire reflection and growth. She radiates love in all she does.

Neve Grace – Ayurveda Lifestyle Coach, Washington DC, USA

Teressa Todd

It is a real and true account of how life keeps throwing curve balls at us, often when we least expect it. I can see this would be an encouraging and inspirational read for anyone going through similar experiences.

Sam Partner – Gold Coast, Australia.

So much motivation, passion and inspiration. Every page makes you want to read more. Teressa's sincere words and brilliant writing made this a must-read! A book that is not just for the eyes, but for holistic well-being.

Arianne Evangelista – Manilla, Philippines

The words courage and bravery, don't even come close to define what Teressa has had to embrace, to truly rise and succeed in her life. What an incredible journey!

Kleo Merrick – Online Business Strategist, Melbourne, Australia

Kitiboni Rolle-Adderley

Definitely inspirational! Excellent read Dr Kiti! You aptly navigated the labyrinth of motherhood, career, family life, and life-long learning. I am drawn to your incredible strength and immersible focus to go after your dreams.

Janet McKenzie, M.S.c. – Superintendent of Police Royal Bahamas Police Force

Dr Adderley's life story is a testament of the proverbial adage, "when life gives you lemons, make lemonade". So many women relate to this and I applaud Dr Adderley for sharing her story with a message of encouragement, optimism, and a positive can-do attitude in the face of adversity. Powerful!

Shannelle DePass – Supervising Senior, Restructuring & Turnaround, Bahamas

I found this to be highly informative and insightful. The vulnerability shown is heartfelt and moving. She would be a recommended choice of mine as a therapist or coach. I for one want to connect to someone who shows their human emotions.

Clayton Phillips – Executive Protection Specialist. Advanced Instructor of Self Defence. Owner, Professional Renaissance Protection Bahamas

Petros Galanoulis

Petros highlights the importance of recognising emotional fatigue and burnout and taking care of your own wellbeing so you can continue to be of service to others. These practical tools will enhance not only your role as a coach but help you thrive at life.

Tara Doherty

Petros highlights an important concept: you need Positive Selfishness. Because if you give it all you can't keep going. It's like having a renewable forest, you need to do the planting and harvest it in stages. If you do it all at once you'll have a lower yield and jeopardise future harvests.

Daniel Monk

Insightful and thought-provoking. Petros eloquently shows us that to perform at our highest levels of "self" the practice of Positive Selfishness is crucial to our wellbeing.

Scott Merrick

www.ingramcontent.com/pod-product-compliance
Lightning Source LLC
Chambersburg PA
CBHW071627080526
44588CB00010B/1299